A Colour Atlas of
Heart Failure

Presented as a service

to medicine

with the compliments of

MSD
MERCK
SHARP&
DOHME

Merck Sharp & Dohme Limited

A Colour Atlas of
HEART FAILURE

Leonard M. Shapiro
MD, MRCP
Senior Registrar, National Heart Hospital, London

Kim M. Fox
MD, MRCP
Consultant Cardiologist, National Heart Hospital, London

Wolfe Medical Publications Limited

Copyright © L.M. Shapiro, K.M. Fox, 1988
Published by Wolfe Medical Publications Ltd, 1988
Printed by Grafos, Arte Sobre Papel, Barcelona, Spain
ISBN 0 7234 0935 8 Cased edition
ISBN 0 7234 1716 4 Limp edition

Reprinted 1991

For a full list of titles published by
Wolfe Medical Publications Ltd, please
write to the publishers at: 2–16 Torrington
Place, London WC1E 7LT, England.

CONTENTS

ACKNOWLEDGEMENTS

We are indebted to the many friends and colleagues who contributed the illustrations for this text. In particular, we acknowledge the help of Mr B. Richards, who provided invaluable help with photography of the figures and Miss Kathy Back, who typed the text. Many of the pathological illustrations were kindly provided by the Reginald Hudson Museum (Curator Dr E. Olsen). We also wish to thank the following who have lent us many illustrations; Dr Carol Warnes, Dr R. Underwood, Dr D. Longmore, Dr M. Rubens, Dr M. Raphael, Dr P. Crean, Professor M. Yacoub, Dr R. Donaldson, Mr G. Castle and Miss Caroline Westgate.

PREFACE

Breathlessness is a common cardiac symptom. This atlas of heart failure contains colour photographs of the pathology and investigation of patients suffering from both the common and uncommon causes of this condition. This book is divided into 8 sections and every attempt has been made to be as comprehensive as possible. This atlas is primarily aimed at undergraduates, postgraduates studying for higher diplomas, physicians and general practitioners, who manage patients with heart disease.

I CLINICAL FEATURES OF HEART FAILURE

Heart failure is usually defined as the inability of the heart to generate an output sufficient to meet the metabolic requirements of the body. The left or right ventricles may fail individually or together. Heart failure may also occur in the face of normal ventricular function.

Left heart failure presents with shortness of breath which, if severe, will occur at rest. The physical signs are those of pulmonary oedema and evidence of myocardial dysfunction such as low output and a gallop rhythm. Occasionally, low cardiac output (fatigue, cool peripheries, shock and organ failure) may occur in the absence of pulmonary congestion. Right heart failure, either secondary to left heart failure or in isolation, will cause an elevated jugular venous pressure and peripheral oedema.

In the clinical examination of a patient with heart failure, it is essential to search for the underlying aetiology since heart failure is not in itself a diagnosis. Important causes include ischaemic heart disease, valvular heart disease, cardiomyopathies, heart muscle disease and hypertension. More rarely, congenital heart lesions, pulmonary embolism, pulmonary hypertension, high output states, pericardial disease and cardiac tumours may precipitate heart failure.

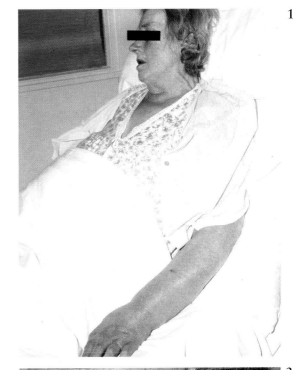

1

1 Patients with left ventricular failure usually present with breathlessness. In the most severe forms breathlessness will occur at rest and be associated with orthopnoea and paroxysmal nocturnal dyspnoea. This patient with congestive cardiac failure was short of breath and orthopnoeic and in addition had peripheral oedema.

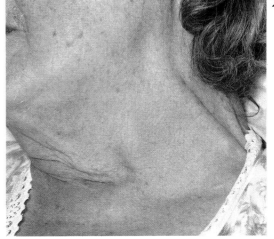

2

2 An elevated jugular venous pressure reflects a raised right atrial pressure which in turn may be due to an elevated right ventricular filling pressure and right heart failure. It is very important when measuring the jugular venous pressure to measure the height of the internal jugular vein, since the external jugular vein may not necessarily reflect true right atrial pressure. Examination of the jugular venous pressure should include an estimation of the A wave and the V wave together with the rate of the X and Y descent.

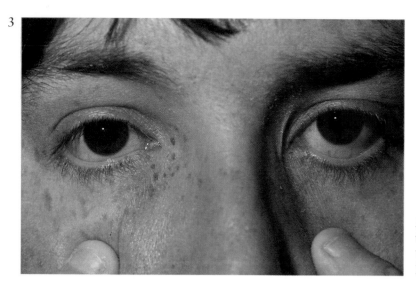

3 When right heart failure is severe, there will be hepatic congestion which will lead to the development of jaundice.

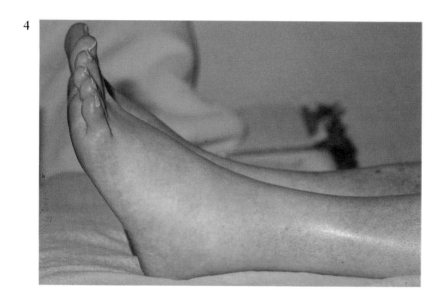

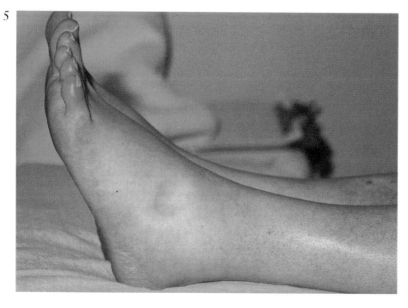

4 & 5 Right heart failure often leads to the development of peripheral oedema (**4**) which is characteristically pitting (**5**).

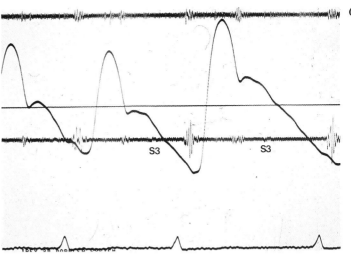

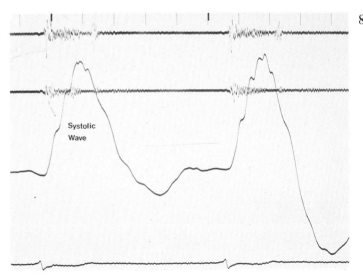

6 & 7 Auscultation in heart failure will usually reveal the presence of a third heart sound (6) or both a third and fourth heart sound (7). Sinus tachycardia associated with heart failure will result in a summation of the third and fourth heart sounds and typically gives rise to a 'gallop' rhythm.

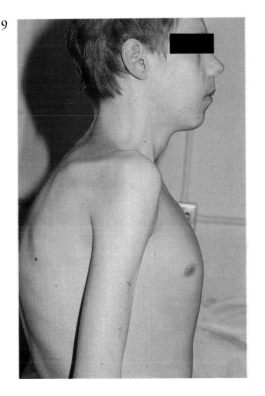

8 An elevated systolic wave of the jugular venous pressure usually indicates the presence of tricuspid regurgitation; this is a frequent accompaniment of right heart failure.

9 Heart failure during the growth period in a child results in marked chest deformity from extreme cardiomegaly. In this example, the chest has an increased anterior-posterior dimension and in addition there is muscle loss.

II ISCHAEMIC HEART DISEASE

Angina Pectoris

During myocardial ischaemia, abnormalities of left ventricular function develop and if sufficiently severe may result in transient left ventricular failure. Alternatively, if the ischaemia involves the papillary muscle, transient mitral regurgitation may occur.

Although most patients, during myocardial ischaemia, will complain of angina pectoris some patients may only complain of shortness of breath, while others may notice the development of both angina and shortness of breath concomitantly.

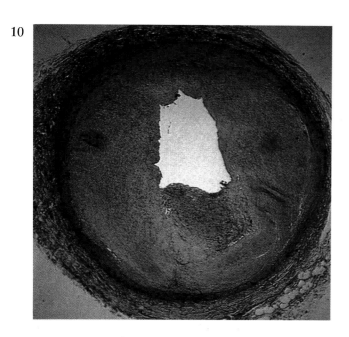

10 Coronary artery narrowed more than 75% in cross sectional area by plaque. This is a significant degree of coronary artery stenosis.

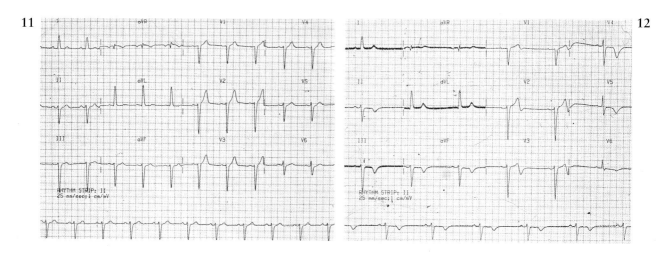

11 & 12 Resting 12 lead electrocardiogram in a patient with a previous anterior myocardial infarction (**11**). During chest pain, the patient developed severe shortness of breath; this was associated with the development of myocardial ischaemia seen on the electrocardiogram as widespread T wave inversion (**12**).

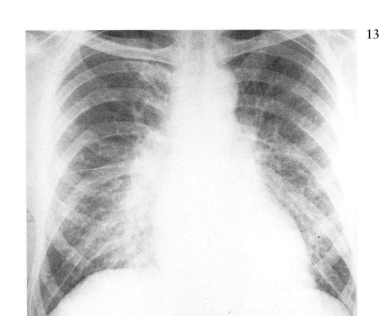

13 Chest radiograph showing a small heart with pulmonary oedema due to the myocardial dysfunction associated with angina pectoris.

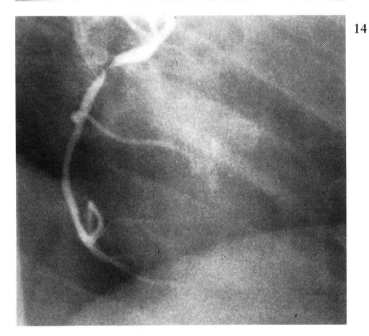

14 Coronary arteriogram (left anterior oblique projection) showing significant atherosclerotic narrowing of the right coronary artery.

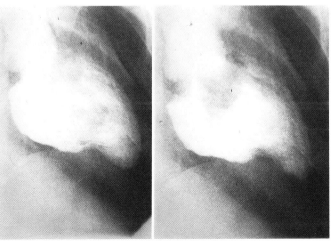

15 Left ventricular angiogram (systole left, diastole right) showing overall good left ventricular function with inferior dyskinesia due to right coronary disease. During angina pectoris, the left ventricular function deteriorated markedly in this patient and he developed heart failure with mitral regurgitation.

Acute Myocardial Infarction

During acute myocardial infarction there is depression of left ventricular function which may lead to the development of left ventricular failure, particularly if the infarct is extensive or if there are complications such as the development of cardiac arrhythmias. Hypertensive and diabetic patients are also particularly at risk. The development of left ventricular failure shortly after acute myocardial infarction is a bad prognostic feature.

16

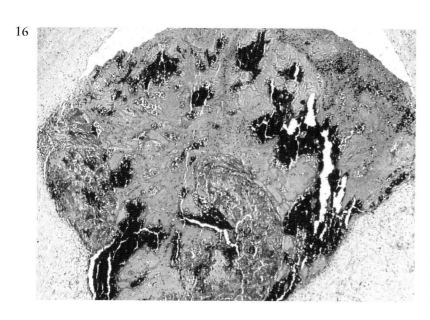

16 Cross section through a coronary artery thrombus. The thrombus consists mainly of platelets interspersed with a few red blood cells and fibrin.

17

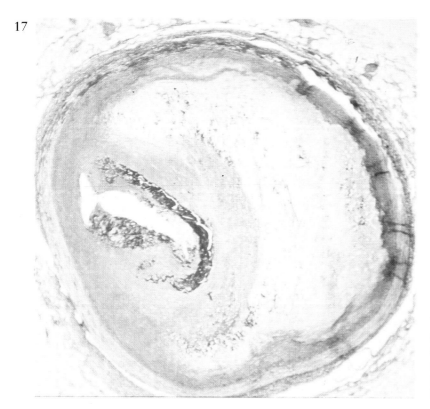

17 Cross section through a left anterior descending coronary artery at the site of thrombus. There is disruption of the superficial layer of the plaque and erythrocytes are seen beneath the surface.

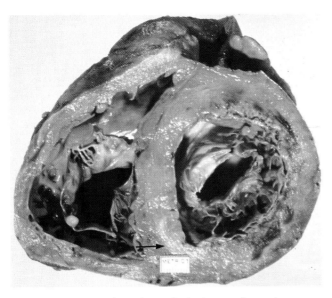

18 Transverse sections through the heart of a patient who had died 6 days after an extensive myocardial infarction. There is extensive necrosis in the anterior wall, the entire lateral wall and extending slightly into the posterior wall. An older white scar is present in the ventricular septum which extends into the posterior wall (arrow). The left ventricular cavity is dilated.

19 Histological section in acute myocardial infarction. There is coagulation necrosis with loss of cell nuclei and infiltration of polymorphonuclear leucocytes.

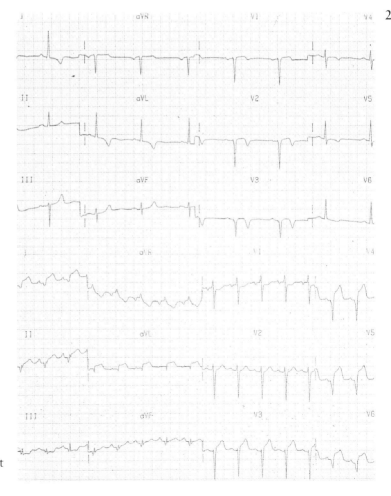

20 Twelve lead electrocardiogram showing (above) an anterior myocardial infarction. Over the succeeding days, the patient developed further chest pain and extended the infarction laterally (below). This was accompanied by the development of acute left ventricular failure.

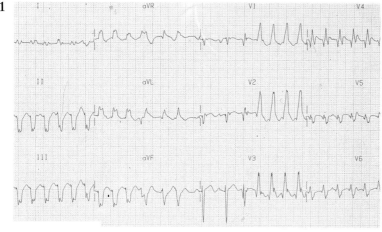

21 Twelve lead electrocardiogram showing ventricular tachycardia in a patient with an acute myocardial infarction. The development of cardiac arrhythmias in patients with acute myocardial infarction often leads to left ventricular failure.

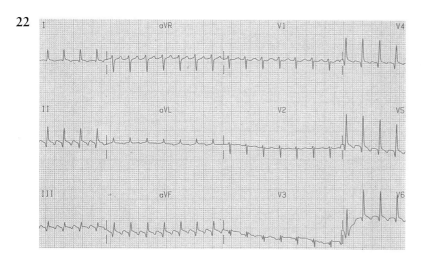

22 Twelve lead electrocardiogram showing the development of atrial flutter in a patient with an acute inferior and lateral myocardial infarction.

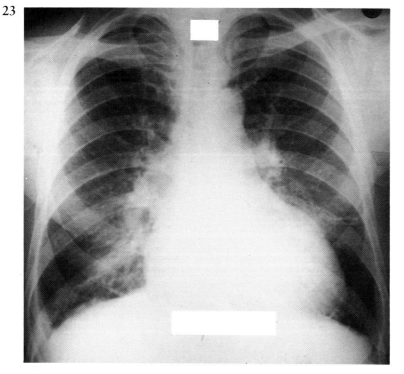

23 Chest radiograph showing a slightly enlarged heart and pulmonary oedema following an acute myocardial infarction.

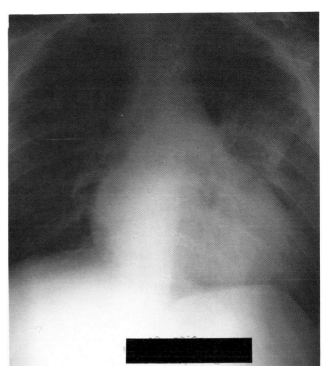

24 Chest radiograph showing that pulmonary oedema though usually generalised throughout the lungs, may be localised.

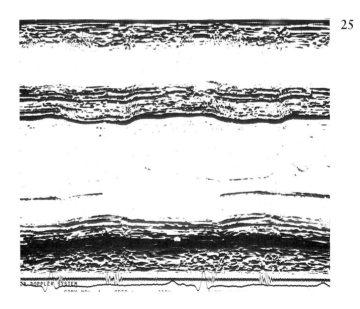

25 M-mode echocardiogram through the left ventricle in myocardial infarction. The left ventricular cavity is dilated and there is poor contraction of both the septum, and in particular, the posterior left ventricular wall.

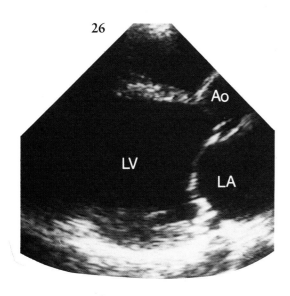

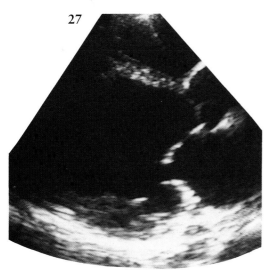

26 & 27 Cross sectional echocardiogram (parasternal long axis view) through the left ventricle in myocardial infarction. A systolic frame (**26**) and diastolic frame (**27**) are shown. There is left ventricular dilatation and poor contraction of the septum and posterior wall. Ao – aorta; LA – left atrium; LV – left ventricle.

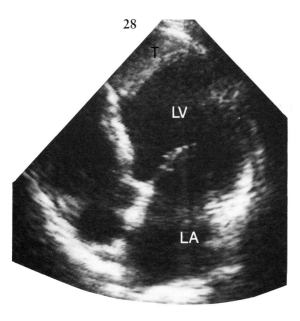

28 Cross sectional echocardiogram (apical long axis view). Following myocardial infarction, particularly in association with heart failure, a left ventricular thrombus may be seen. In this example, there is laminar thrombus (T) at the apex of the left ventricle (LV). LA – left atrium.

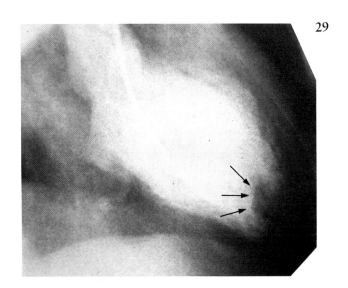

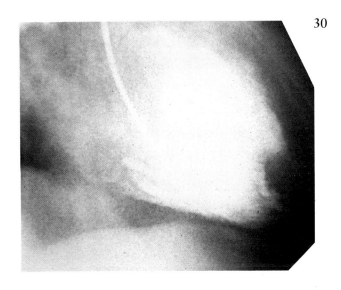

29 & 30 Left ventricular angiogram (systole **29**, diastole **30**) showing poor left ventricular function with an apical filling defect due to left ventricular thrombus (arrows).

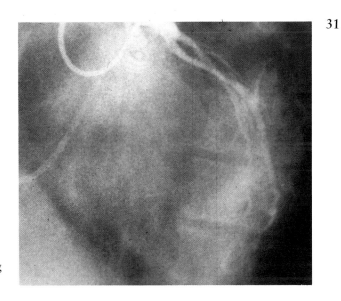

31 Coronary arteriogram (left anterior oblique projection). In patients with myocardial infarction, occlusion of the coronary arteries is the most common finding. In this example, there is complete occlusion without collateralisation of the left anterior descending coronary artery.

Early complications of acute myocardial infarction – mitral regurgitation

The development of mitral regurgitation following acute myocardial infarction is very frequently associated with left ventricular failure. It usually occurs in the setting of inferior myocardial infarction which involves a papillary muscle. The amount of myocardial damage may be very limited.

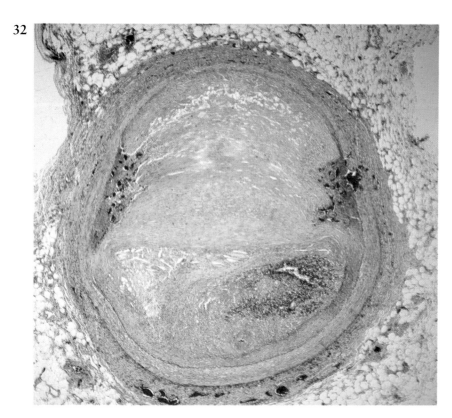

32 Cross section of an occluded right coronary artery.

33 Excised mitral valve showing rupture of the papillary muscle.

34 Excised mitral valve showing ischaemic scarring of the papillary muscle (arrows).

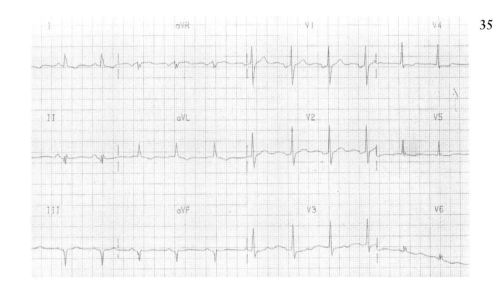

35 Twelve lead electrocardiogram showing inferior myocardial infarction which extends posteriorly.

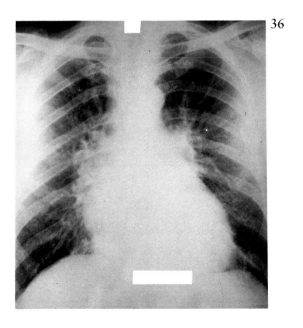

36 Chest radiograph showing a slightly enlarged heart with obvious pulmonary oedema in a patient who developed mitral regurgitation following acute myocardial infarction.

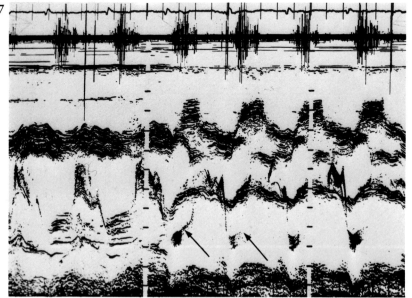

37 M-mode echocardiographic sweep from the left ventricle to the aortic root. The mitral valve on the left of the figure is shown to be thick and vibrating and the scan towards the aortic root shows the valve is displaced backwards into the left atrium (arrows) during systole due to prolapse of a flail valve.

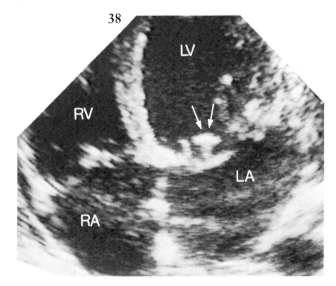

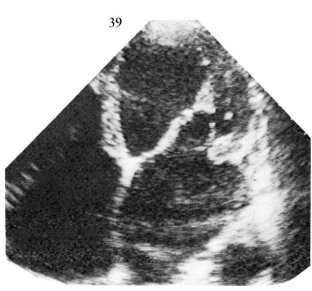

38 & 39 Cross sectional echocardiogram (apical four chamber view; systole **38**, diastole **39**). The mitral valve can be seen to be prolapsing into the left atrium and there are ruptured chordae attached to the valve (arrows). Left ventricular function is moderately impaired. LA – left atrium; LV – left ventricle; RA – right atrium; RV – right ventricle.

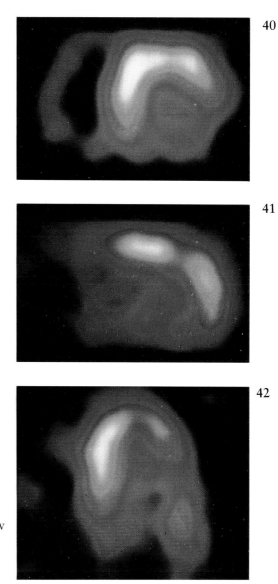

40-42 Thallium tomographic scans (short axis view **40**, vertical long axis view **41**, horizontal long axis view **42**) showing a defect in the uptake of thallium involving the inferior and lateral wall of the left ventricle.

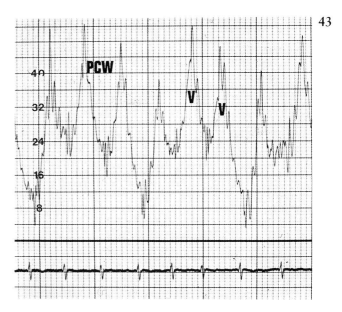

43 Haemodynamics in mitral regurgitation following acute myocardial infarction shows a very high V wave in the wedge pressure tracing.

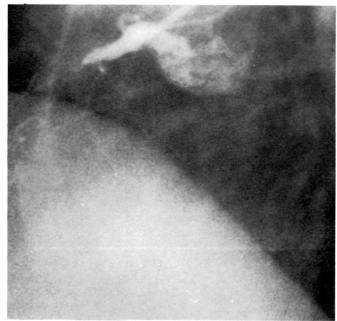

44 Coronary arteriogram (left anterior oblique projection) showing a blocked right coronary artery.

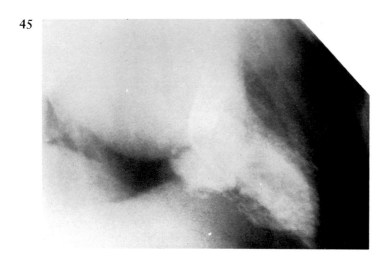

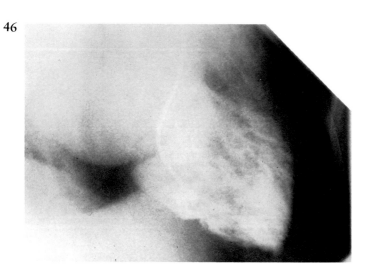

45 & 46 Left ventricular angiogram (systole **45**, diastole **46**) showing inferior dyskinesia and gross mitral regurgitation due to papillary muscle dysfunction. The overall left ventricular function is well preserved.

Early complications of acute myocardial infarction – ventricular septal defect

Ventricular septal defect is an uncommon but well known complication of acute myocardial infarction. When it occurs it is usually large and rapidly leads to the development of left ventricular failure and a low output state. Ventricular septal defect is usually due to occlusion of the left anterior descending coronary artery though occasionally it can result from inferior infarction. It is often clinically difficult to distinguish from acute mitral regurgitation.

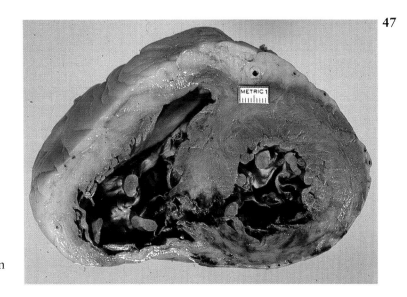

47 Section through the posterior part of the septum showing a large ventricular septal defect that occurred secondary to an acute myocardial infarction.

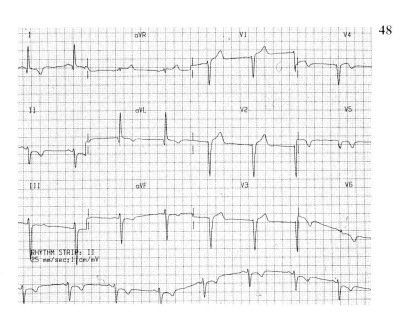

48 Electrocardiogram in ventricular septal defect usually shows an anteroseptal myocardial infarction.

49

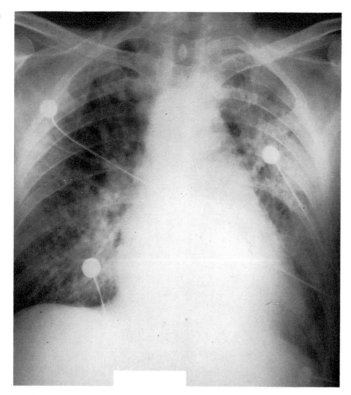

49 Chest x-ray in ventricular septal defect showing pulmonary plethora and an enlarged heart.

50

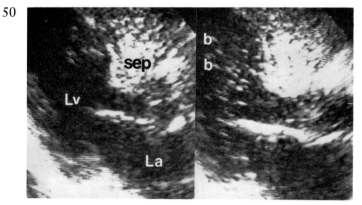

50 Cross sectional echocardiogram (parasternal long axis view). On the right the echocardiogram is shown following a ventricular septal defect. On the left, following an injection of agitated saline into the right ventricle, passage of contrast as microbubbles (b) into the left ventricle (LV) confirms the presence of a left to right shunt at ventricular level. La – left atrium; sep – septum.

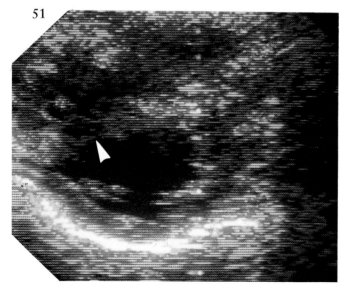

51 Cross sectional echocardiogram (parasternal short axis view). In this view a ventricular septal defect can be seen (arrow).

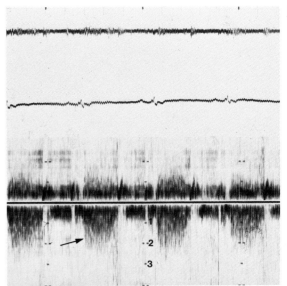

52 Continuous wave Doppler (apical view). There is a high velocity jet (arrow) confirming the presence of a ventricular septal defect.

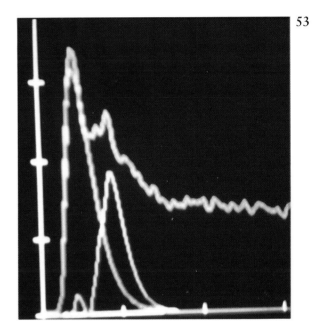

53 First pass radionuclide angiocardiogram showing pulmonary activity time curve (yellow) and gamma fits to the main and recirculation peaks (green and pink respectively). From the area under the green and pink curves, the pulmonary systemic flow ratio can be calculated which in this example is greater than 3:1.

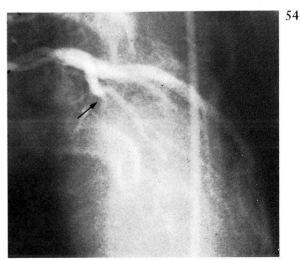

54 Coronary arteriogram (left anterior oblique projection) showing a blocked left anterior descending coronary artery (arrow).

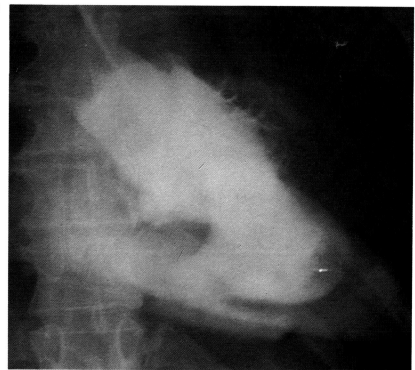

55 Left ventriculogram (postero-anterior projection) showing filling of both the left and right ventricles from the left ventricle.

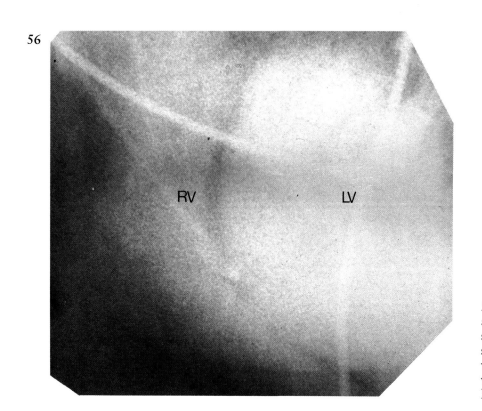

56 Left ventriculogram (left anterior oblique projection) showing a large ventricular septal defect with filling of both ventricles from the left ventricle. LV– left ventricle; RV– right ventricle.

Late complications of acute myocardial infarction – left ventricular aneurysm

The development of a left ventricular aneurysm following acute myocardial infarction is an important cause of heart failure. Heart failure may occur weeks, months or even occasionally years after the acute myocardial infarction. The site of the aneurysm is either anterior or inferior and classically shows persistent ST segment elevation on the electrocardiogram with a bulge noted on the chest x-ray; however these abnormalities may not necessarily be evident. Very rarely blunt chest trauma may lead to the development of a left ventricular aneurysm. In a patient with a left ventricular aneurysm, cardiac arrhythmias, particularly ventricular tachycardia are an important complication that may exacerbate or precipitate heart failure. The diagnosis is best made using gated blood pool imaging and left ventricular angiography which not only allows definition of the aneurysm to be made but also permits the viability of the remaining myocardium to be assessed. This may be important if surgical resection is to be considered.

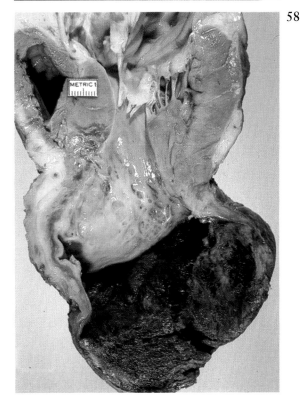

57

58

57 Macroscopic view (longitudinal section) of the heart. There is a thin area of myocardial scar at the apex which caused aneurysm formation.

58 Macroscopic section (echocardiographic long axis cut) showing a huge left ventricular aneurysm with laminated thrombus within it.

59

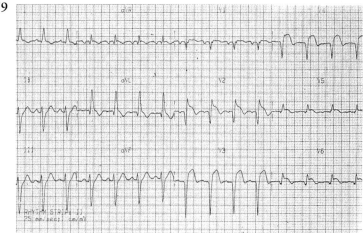

60

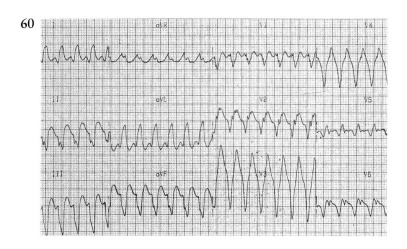

59 & 60 Electrocardiograms in sinus rhythm (**59**) and during ventricular tachycardia (**60**) in left ventricular aneurysm. The 12 lead electrocardiogram in sinus rhythm shows an old anterior myocardial infarction with persistent ST segment elevation. Ventricular tachycardia is an important complication which may precipitate pulmonary oedema.

61

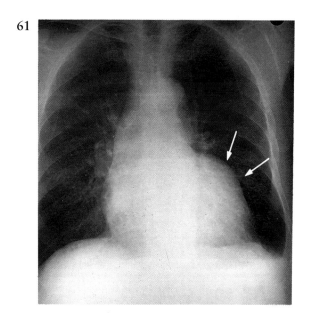

62

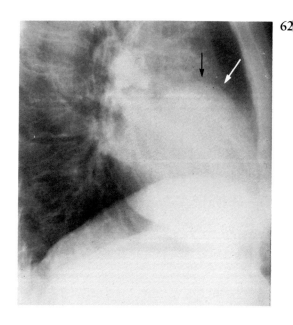

61 & 62 Chest radiograph (postero-anterior projection **61**, lateral projection **62**) showing a bulge (arrows) on the left ventricular border of the heart which is seen to be anteriorly situated on the lateral view due to a left ventricular aneurysm.

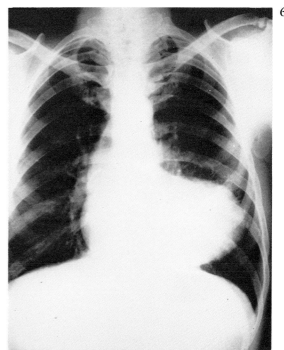

63 Chest radiograph showing a localised bulge, due to an antero-apical aneurysm.

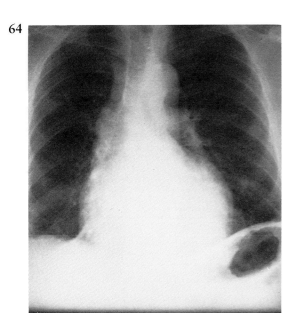

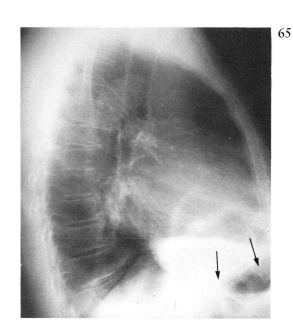

64 & 65 Chest radiograph (postero-anterior projection **64**, lateral projection **65**) showing inferior calcification in an inferior aneurysm (arrows).

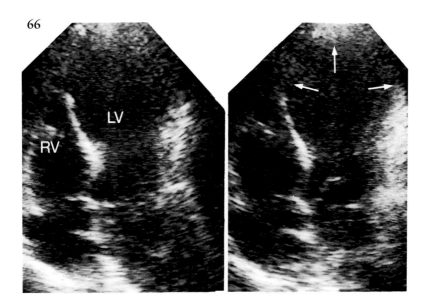

66 Cross sectional echocardiogram (apical four chamber view; systole right, diastole left). A large apical aneurysm (arrows) is seen in which there is no contraction compared with the base of the left ventricle. LV – left ventricle; RV – right ventricle.

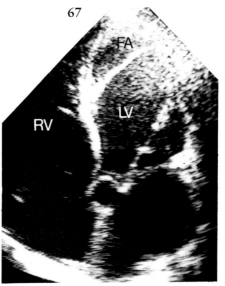

67 Cross sectional echocardiogram (apical four chamber view) showing a false aneurysm (Fa) of the left ventricular apex which may be seen as a fluid filled space. LV – left ventricle; RV – right ventricle.

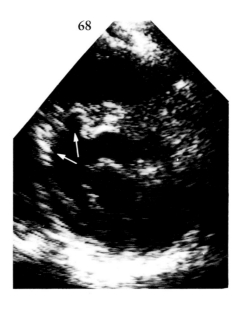

68 Cross sectional echocardiogram (parasternal short axis view). A well localised septal aneurysm may be seen (arrowed).

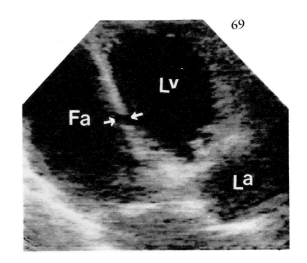

69 Cross sectional echocardiogram (apical two chamber view). Occasionally false aneurysms (Fa) of the left ventricle may occur and, as in this example, free communication between the left ventricle and a fibrous lined sac can be seen. La – left atrium; Lv – left ventricle.

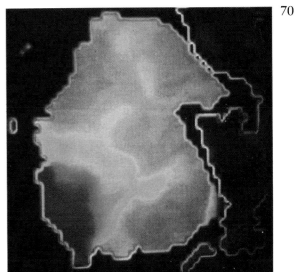

70 & 71 Gated blood pool imaging in left ventricular aneurysm (pre-operatively **70**, post-operatively after resection of the aneurysm **71**). These are amplitude images and a large area of the apex is not contracting (in dark red on the image). After resection of the aneurysm, this area of akinesis is no longer evident.

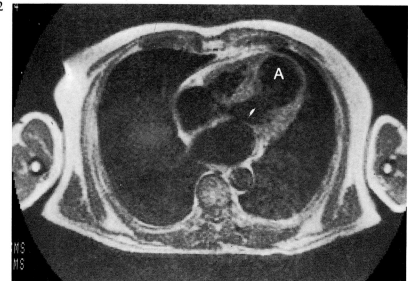

72 Magnetic resonance image (saggital section) showing a thin area at the apex in left ventricular aneurysmal formation (A).

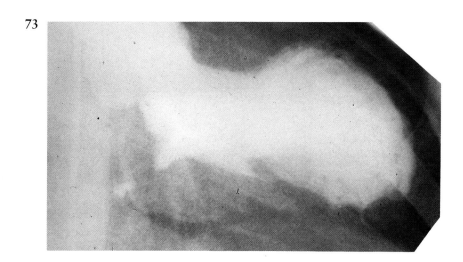

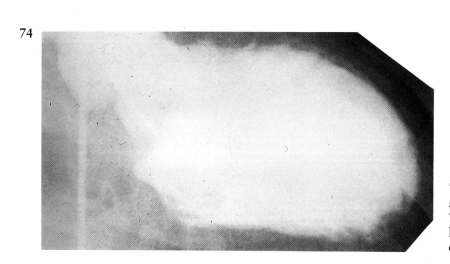

73 & 74 Left ventricular angiogram (systole **73**, diastole **74**) showing a large antero-apical left ventricular aneurysm evident on the systolic frame.

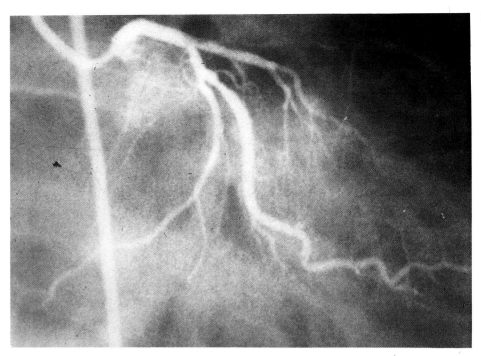

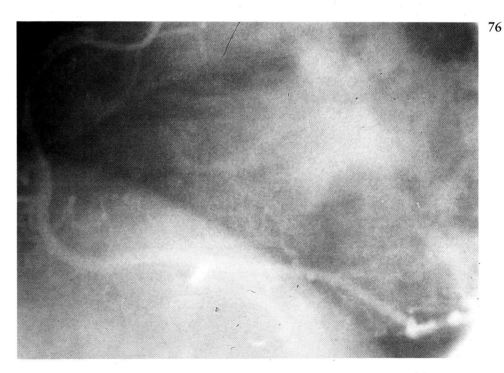

75 & 76 Coronary arteriogram (left coronary artery in the right anterior oblique projection **75**; right coronary artery in the left anterior oblique projection **76**). The left anterior descending coronary artery is completely blocked and injection of the right coronary artery shows that there is no retrograde filling of this vessel.

Late complications of acute myocardial infarction – extensive myocardial damage

Left ventricular failure may occur late after one or more myocardial infarctions. This is usually due to extensive myocardial damage. Except for the presence of coronary disease on angiography, this condition is indistinguishable from dilated cardiomyopathy. Usually, there would be multivessel coronary artery disease but this is not always the case.

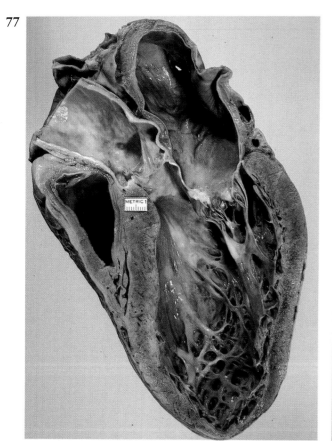 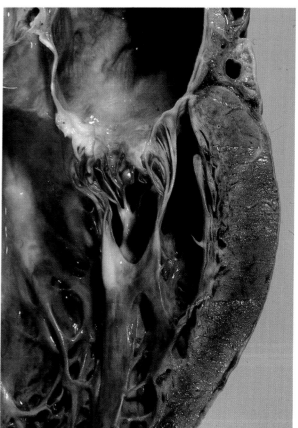

77 & 78 Macroscopic section (echo cut; low power view **77**, higher power view **78**) showing extensive myocardial scarring with thinning of the myocardium.

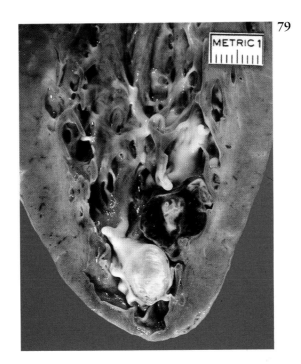

79 Macroscopic section (longitudinal view) showing calcified thrombus in the left ventricle in the presence of extensive myocardial damage with fibrosis.

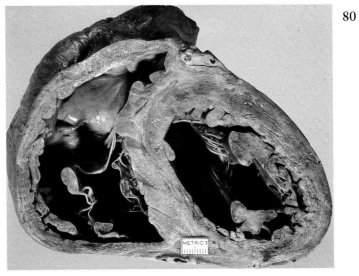

80 Macroscopic section (cross sectional echo cut) showing widespread myocardial damage.

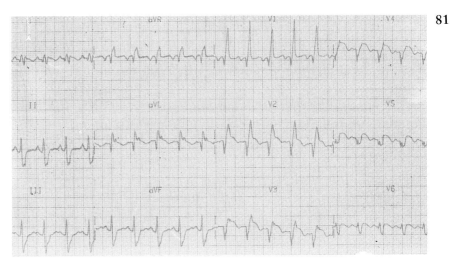

81 Electrocardiogram in heart failure due to extensive myocardial damage. This shows anterior infarction with right bundle branch block. The development of bundle branch block following anterior myocardial infarction nearly always indicates widespread damage.

82

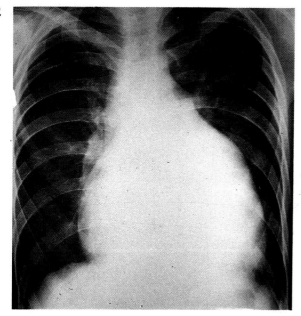

82 Chest radiograph showing a grossly enlarged heart following multiple previous infarctions.

83

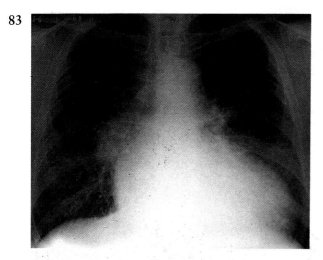

83 Chest radiograph showing an enlarged heart and pulmonary oedema.

84

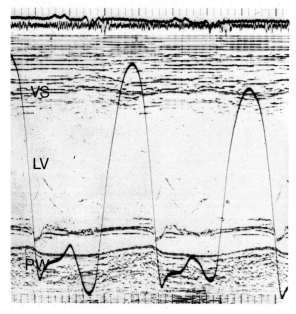

84 M-mode echocardiogram showing a left ventricle (LV) that is grossly dilated and contracts poorly. PW – posterior wall; VS – ventricular septum.

85 Cross sectional echocardiogram (parasternal long axis view). The diastolic frame (right) shows a dilated left ventricle (LV) with thinning of the ventricular septum. The systolic frame (left) shows poor contraction of both the septum and posterior wall. Ao – aorta; LA – left atrium; LV – left ventricle.

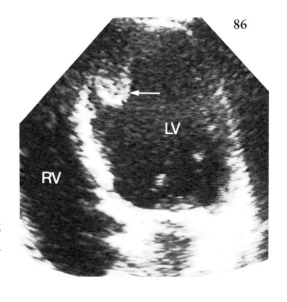

86 Cross sectional echocardiogram (apical four chamber view). The development of left ventricular thrombus is frequently seen in this condition. In this example there is a large fusiform thrombus (arrow) arising at the apex of the left ventricle (LV) extending into the cavity. RV – right ventricle.

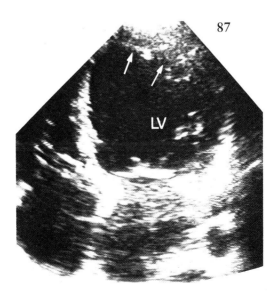

87 Cross sectional echocardiogram (apical four chamber view). In this example there is a laminated apical thrombus (arrows). LV – left ventricle.

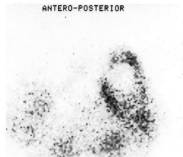
ANTERO-POSTERIOR

LEFT LATERAL

LEFT ANTERIOR OBLIQUE

88 Thallium scintigram showing widespread defects in uptake at rest involving the anterior, septal and apical portions of the left ventricle.

89

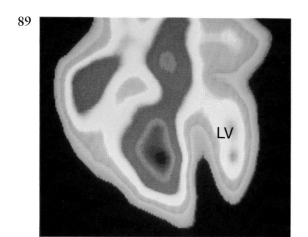

90

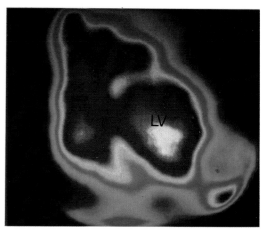

89 & 90 Gated blood pool images showing a normal left ventricle (**89**) and a grossly dilated left ventricle (**90**) in a patient with ischaemic cardiac damage. LV – left ventricle.

91

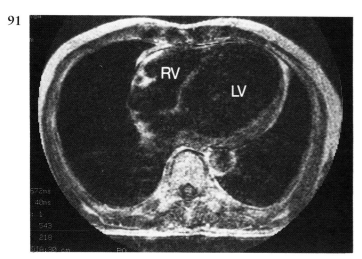

91 Magnetic resonance scan showing a dilated and thinned ventricle in ischaemic heart disease. LV – left ventricle; RV – right ventricle.

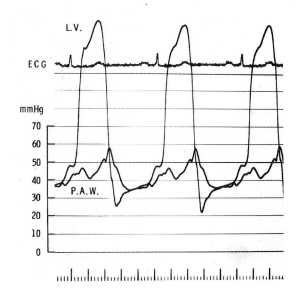

92 Haemodynamic tracing showing a markedly elevated left ventricular end-diastolic and left atrial pressure.

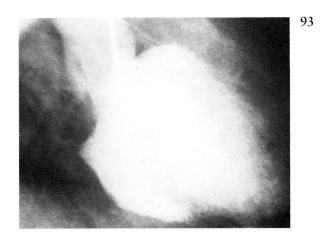

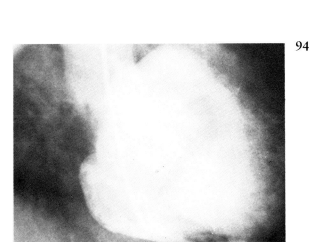

93 & 94 Left ventricular angiogram (systole **93**, diastole **94**). The left ventricular function is extremely poor.

95

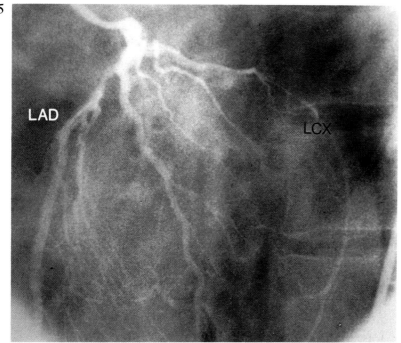

LAD

LCX

96

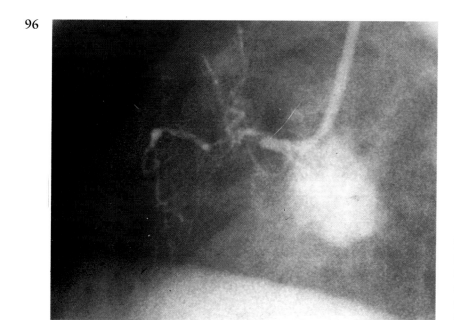

95 & 96 Coronary arteriogram (left coronary artery **95**, right coronary artery **96**). There is severe three vessel coronary artery disease. LAD – left anterior descending; LCX – left circumflex.

III VALVULAR HEART DISEASE

Acute valve disease – infective endocarditis

Infective endocarditis is an important complication of valvular heart disease. It may occur even in the presence of only mild abnormalities of the valves causing them to become severely regurgitant. Rarely, vegetations may produce stenosis. The diagnosis of infective endocarditis must always be considered in any patient who presents with non-specific symptoms or a pyrexia and who has an underlying valve lesion. With the development of severe regurgitation, heart failure develops rapidly. The diagnosis is best made from a combination of haematological investigations, blood cultures plus the clinical stigmata associated with infective endocarditis. The most useful investigation is usually an echocardiogram which may show the presence of a vegetation. However, it is important to be aware that endocarditis may be present even when blood cultures are negative (particularly if antibiotics have been given) or in the absence of vegetations seen on echocardiography.

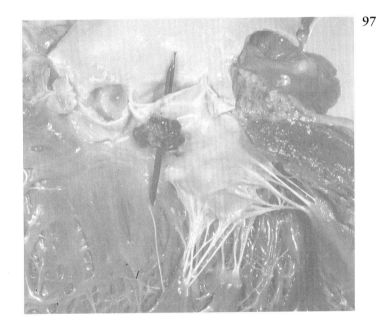

97

97 Infective endocarditis of the aortic valve. The non-affected portions of the cusps appear normal.

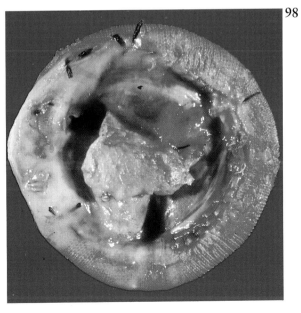

98

98 Vegetation on a xenograft mitral valve in a patient with streptococcal viridans endocarditis.

99

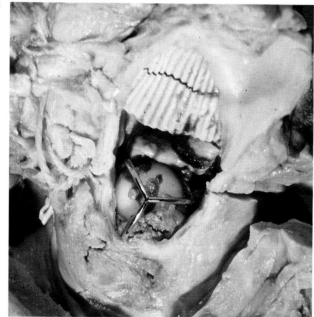

99 Vegetations around the sewing ring of a Starr-Edwards aortic valve.

100

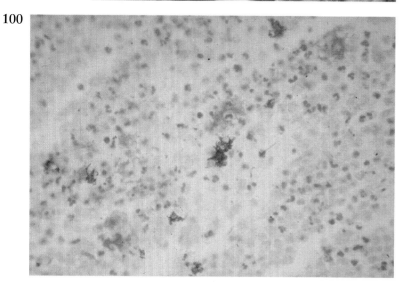

100 Microscopic section showing an infected splenic infarct from the same patient as **99**.

101

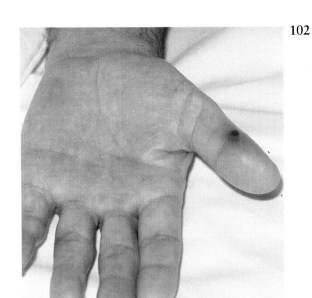

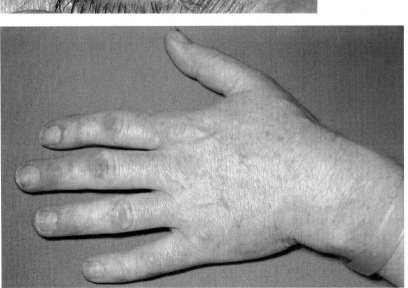

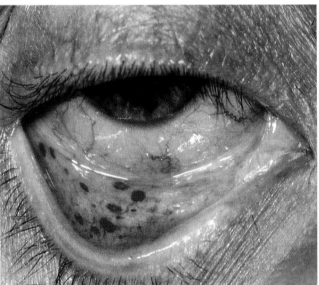

101-104 The physical stigmata of infective endocarditis include splinter haemorrhages (**101**) and finger clubbing, Osler's nodes (**102**), subconjunctival haemorrhage (**103**) and a peripheral vasculitis (**104**).

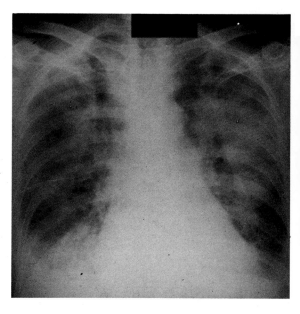

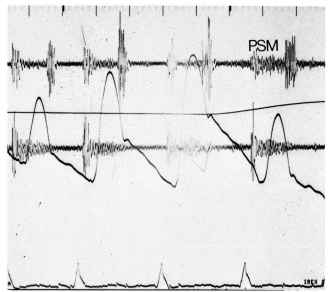

105 Phonocardiogram, electrocardiogram and carotid pulse showing atrial fibrillation, a pansystolic murmur (PSM) and a short ejection time due to heart failure in mitral regurgitation from infective endocarditis, causing ruptured chordae.

106 Chest radiograph showing pulmonary oedema due to acute mitral regurgitation secondary to infective endocarditis.

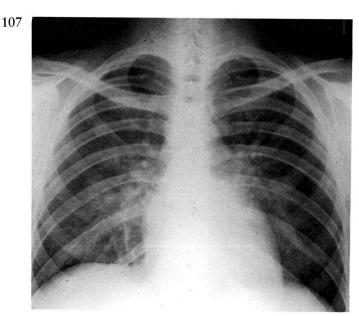

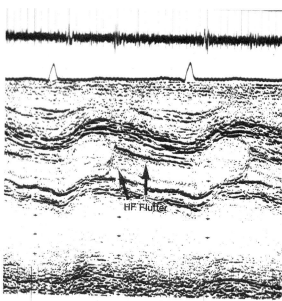

107 Chest radiograph in pulmonary oedema due to acute aortic regurgitation secondary to infective endocarditis. The pulmonary oedema is less florid than in the previous example (**106**).

108 M-mode echocardiogram through the aortic root showing thickening of the aortic valve leaflets, and a high frequency (HF) flutter can be seen in diastole. This is a specific sign of cusp perforation and usually occurs in infective endocarditis.

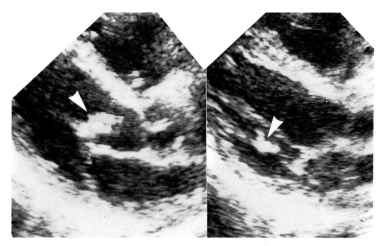

109 Cross sectional
echocardiogram (parasternal
long axis view). On the right, a
diastolic frame is shown with a
large vegetation attached to the
chordae of the anterior leaflet
of the mitral valve. In systole
(left), movement of this
vegetation can be seen (arrow).

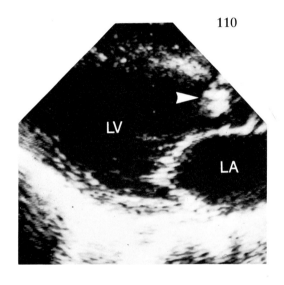

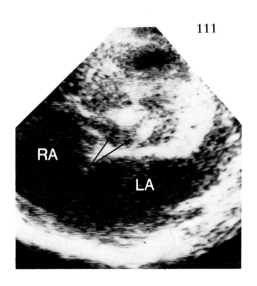

110 & 111 Cross sectional
echocardiogram (parasternal
long axis view **110**, short axis
view **111**). In the long axis view
a vegetation is seen (arrows)
attached to an abnormal
looking aortic valve and in the
short axis view, this can be seen
attached to both cusps of a
bicuspid aortic valve. LA – left
atrium; LV – left ventricle; RA
– right atrium.

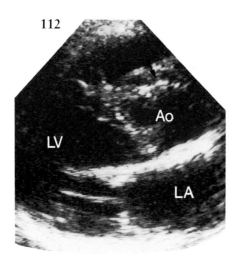

112 Cross sectional echocardiogram (parasternal long axis view). Aortic root abscess is not an uncommon finding in aortic valve endocarditis and in this example there is a fluid filled space anterior to the aortic root (arrow) which at surgery was confirmed to be an abscess cavity. Ao – aorta; LA – left atrium; LV – left ventricle.

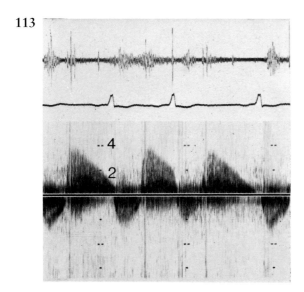

113 Continuous wave Doppler (apical view). Aortic regurgitation which occurs following endocarditis is often acute and severe. In this example there is a low end-diastolic pressure gradient across the aortic valve reflecting the severity of the regurgitation and the high left ventricular end-diastolic pressure.

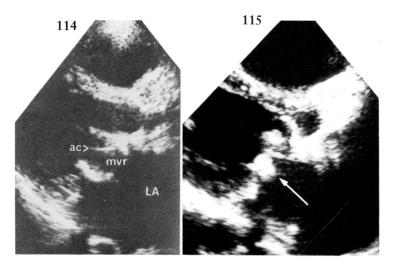

114 & 115 Cross sectional echocardiogram (parasternal long axis view). This shows the findings of a normal mitral valve xenograft (**114**) to be compared with a large vegetation (arrow) seen attached to the xenograft cusps in a man with prosthetic valve endocarditis (**115**). ac – aortic cusp of mitral xenograph; LA – left atrium; mvr – mitral valve replacement.

116 Cross sectional echocardiogram (parasternal long axis view) in systole (left) and diastole (right). In the presence of a mitral valve or aortic valve Starr-Edwards prosthesis it is almost impossible to determine the presence of vegetations because of the echo density of the valve (V).

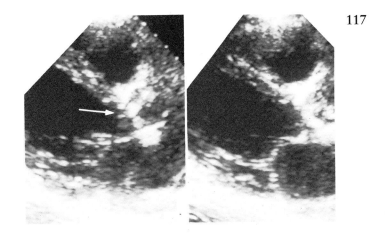

117 Cross sectional echocardiogram (parasternal long axis view). The systolic frame (right) shows prolapse of a flail homograft aortic valve replacement (arrow) due to endocarditis.

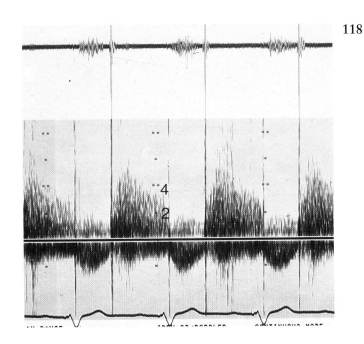

118 Continuous wave Doppler (apical view). Aortic regurgitation is a major complication of infective endocarditis of valve replacements and can be readily detected by Doppler echocardiography.

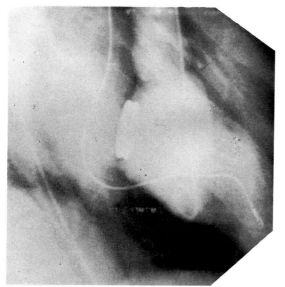
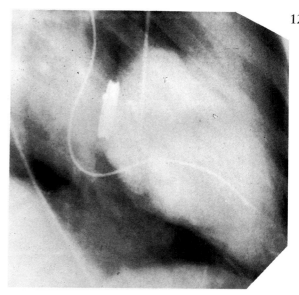

119 & 120 Left ventricular angiogram (systole **119**, diastole **120**) showing severe mitral regurgitation which occurred due to infective endocarditis destroying the seating of a Björk-Shiley mitral valve replacement.

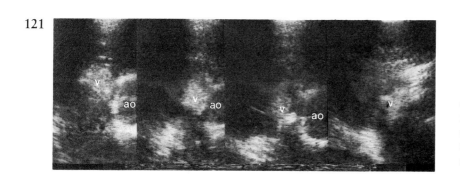

121 Cross sectional echocardiogram (composite apical four chamber view) showing the movement of a vegetation (v) on the tricuspid valve in a drug addict. Ao – aorta.

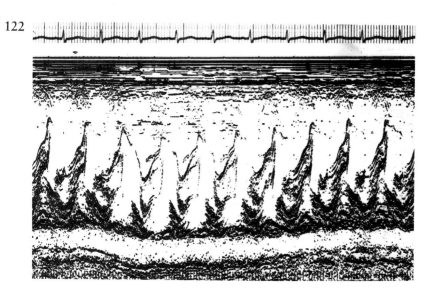

122 M-mode echocardiogram showing a tricuspid vegetation in a drug addict.

Acute valve disease – aortic dissection

Aortic dissection is an uncommon condition and when it involves the ascending aorta and aortic valve it may lead to severe acute aortic regurgitation. In such circumstances, heart failure will often develop. If, in addition, the coronary arteries are involved, acute myocardial infarction will occur and this will further compromise left ventricular function. The diagnosis of acute dissection and heart failure can be readily made from the clinical findings of newly developed aortic regurgitation in a patient presenting with chest pain. The diagnosis can most effectively be made non-invasively using computed tomography. Echocardiography may be helpful. These patients usually require urgent surgery.

123

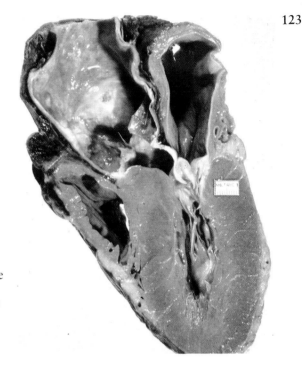

123-125 Long axis section of the heart of an 86-year-old man with aortic dissection (**123**). The ascending aorta is dilated with atherosclerosis. Macroscopic view of the ascending aorta showing an intimal tear (arrow), 3 cm above the coronary ostia, which begins the aortic dissection (**124**), thrombus can be seen within the false channel. Macroscopic view of the right atrioventricular sulcus showing extension of the haemorrhage to the base of the right ventricle (arrow) around the right coronary artery (**125**).

4

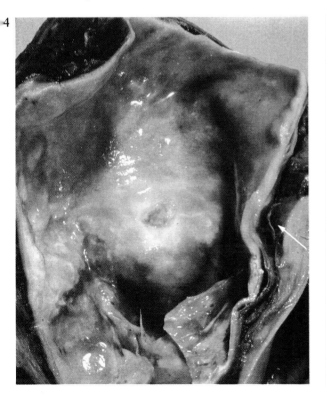

125

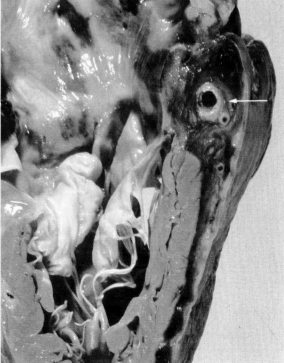

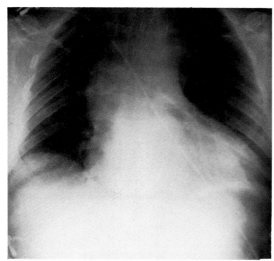

126 Chest radiograph showing dilatation of the aorta associated with dissection.

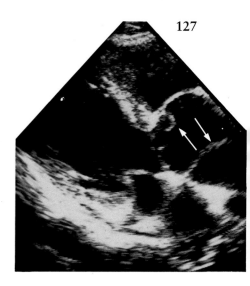

127 Cross sectional echocardiogram (parasternal long axis view) showing aortic dissection. The flap of the dissection may be seen both anteriorly and posteriorly (arrowed) and there is a huge aortic root.

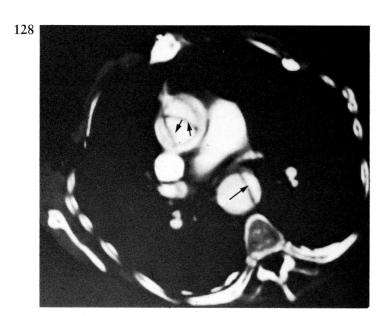

128 Computed tomographic scan of aortic dissection. The flaps (arrowed) can be seen both in the ascending and descending aorta.

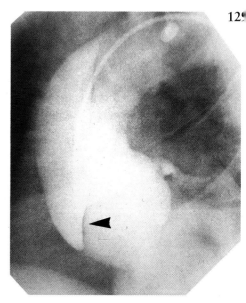

129 Aortogram (left anterior oblique projection) showing the origin of the aortic flap anteriorly (arrow) in the ascending aorta with the dissection involving the aortic valve and causing aortic regurgitation.

Chronic aortic valve disease

Aortic stenosis and aortic regurgitation are important causes of heart failure. The commonest cause of aortic valve disease is a congenital bicuspid aortic valve which subsequently degenerates usually becoming stenotic but occasionally becoming regurgitant. In the older age group, degeneration of a three cusp valve is a common finding leading to both stenosis and regurgitation. Rare causes of aortic valve disease, usually causing aortic regurgitation include Marfan's syndrome, ankylosing spondylitis, Reiter's syndrome, syphilis and the Ehlers Danlos syndrome.

Rheumatic heart disease is an important cause of valvular heart disease but uncommonly involves the aortic valve alone. Usually, the mitral valve is involved as well.

Aortic stenosis of any cause gives similar physical signs, i.e. ejection systolic murmur, slow rising pulse with evidence of left ventricular hypertrophy and, if the valve is bicuspid, a systolic click may be heard. The various causes of aortic stenosis may be differentiated most conveniently by echocardiography.

Aortic regurgitation gives similar physical signs regardless of its aetiology; these include an early diastolic murmur, collapsing pulse and evidence of left ventricular enlargement. There may be other physical signs to suggest the aetiology. Echocardiography is again the investigation of choice for identifying the underlying cause.

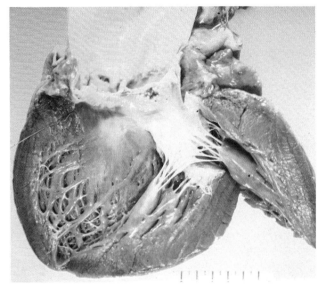

130

130 Aortic stenosis with a calcified valve and left ventricular hypertrophy.

131

131 Macroscopic section of a stenosed bicuspid aortic valve.

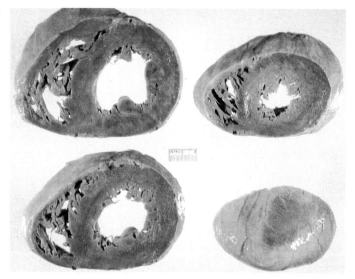

132 Serial macroscopic sections through the heart showing gross hypertrophy of the left ventricle in aortic stenosis.

133

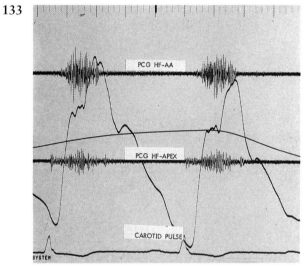

133 Phonocardiogram and carotid pulse in aortic stenosis showing an ejection systolic murmur, absence of A2 and a slow notched upstroke of the pulse.

134

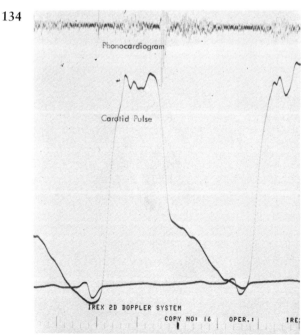

134 Phonocardiogram and carotid pulse in aortic regurgitation showing an ejection systolic murmur, early diastolic murmur and collapsing pulse.

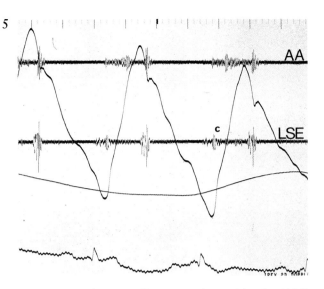

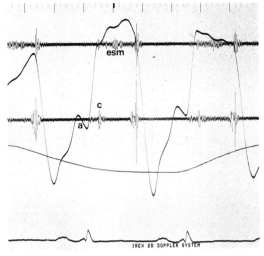

135 & 136 Phonocardiogram and carotid pulse (**135**) and apex cardiogram (**136**) in aortic stenosis with left ventricular failure. There is an ejection click (c) and ejection systolic murmur with a slow rising and ill sustained pulse; there is also a tall a wave with a sustained systolic wave on the apex cardiogram.

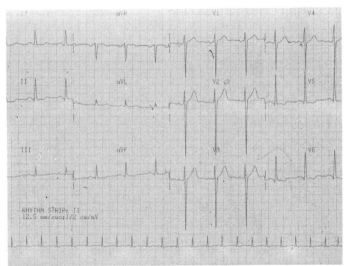

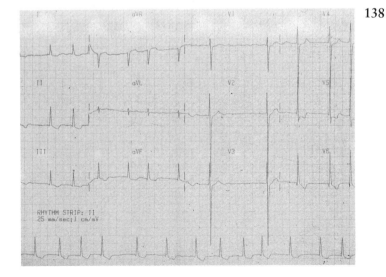

137 & 138 Electrocardiogram in aortic stenosis showing left ventricular hypertrophy with strain (**137**). Subsequently, the patient went into atrial fibrillation with the development of heart failure (**138**).

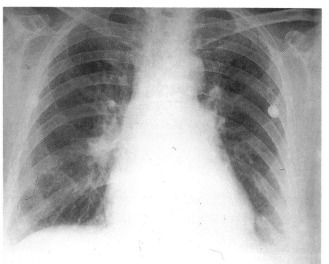

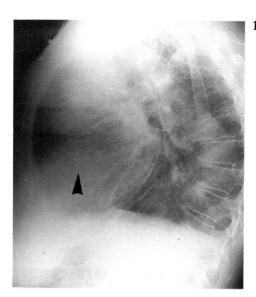

139 & 140 Chest radiograph (postero-anterior projection **139**, lateral projection **140**) in calcific aortic stenosis showing calcium in the aortic valve (arrow). This patient was also in heart failure and there is cardiomegaly and evidence of pulmonary venous congestion.

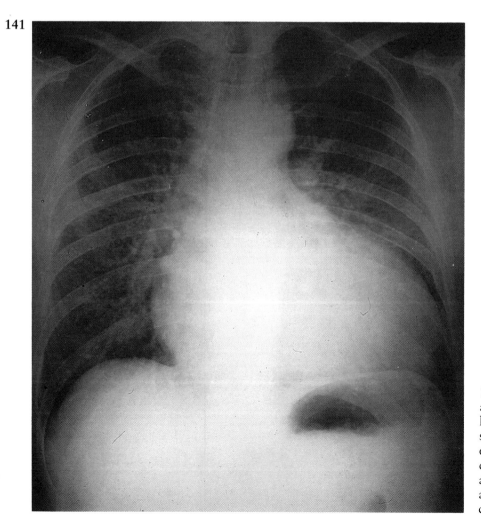

141 Chest radiograph in aortic regurgitation with left ventricular failure showing a grossly enlarged heart with dilatation of the ascending aorta. There is also pulmonary venous congestion.

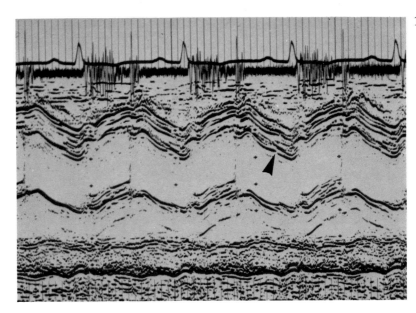

142

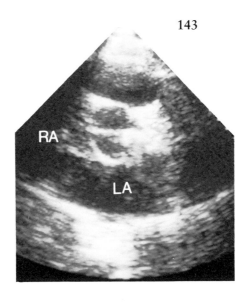

143

142 & 143 M-mode (**142**) and cross sectional echocardiogram (**143**) showing a bicuspid aortic valve. The M-mode echocardiogram through the aortic valve and root shows an eccentric valve closure line (arrow). The cross sectional echocardiogram confirms the presence of two aortic valve cusps with a horizontal closure line. LA – left atrium; RA – right atrium.

144

144 M-mode echocardiogram in calcific aortic stenosis. With calcification, the aortic valve features are lost on echocardiography. Ao – aorta; LA – left atrium; RV – right ventricle.

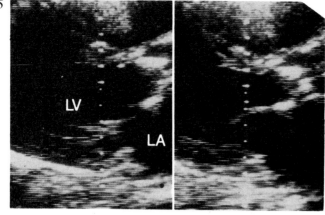

145 Cross sectional echocardiogram (parasternal long axis view). In systole (left) upward doming of the thickened calcified valve may be seen compared with the diastolic frame (right). LA – left atrium; LV – left ventricle.

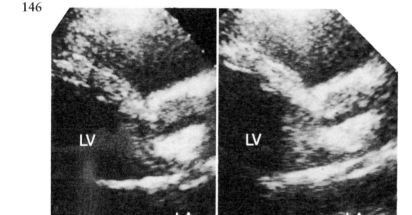

146 Cross sectional echocardiogram (parasternal long axis view). With severe calcification, no valvular motion is apparent. LA – left atrium; LV – left ventricle.

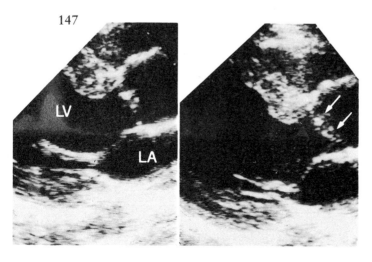

147 Cross sectional echocardiogram (parasternal long axis view). In aortic regurgitation, the aortic valve may appear normal with aortic root dilatation. Occasionally, aortic valve prolapse may be seen as in this example (arrows). The diastolic frame (right) shows aortic valve prolapse compared with the systolic frame (left). LA – left atrium; LV – left ventricle.

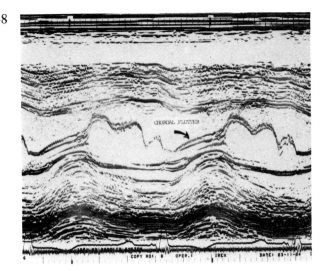

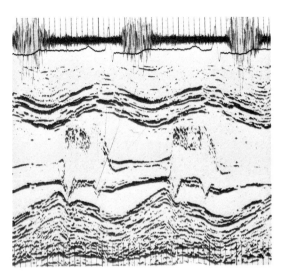

148 M-mode echocardiogram through the left ventricle. There is left ventricular hypertrophy with a small left ventricular cavity. This reflects the presence of severe aortic stenosis and in addition, there is chordal flutter suggesting the presence of mild aortic regurgitation.

149 M-mode echocardiogram through the left ventricle. In aortic stenosis, heart failure may ensue without left ventricular dilatation. In this example, there is gross thickening of the posterior wall with abnormal left ventricular function without cavity dilatation. There is, in addition, mitral valve flutter reflecting aortic regurgitation.

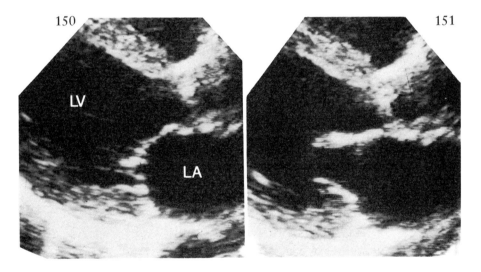

150 & 151 Cross sectional echocardiogram (parasternal long axis view) in systole (**150**) and diastole (**151**). With the onset of heart failure in aortic stenosis, left ventricular hypertrophy is still present, but contraction of the left ventricle is poor as in this example. LA – left atrium; LV – left ventricle.

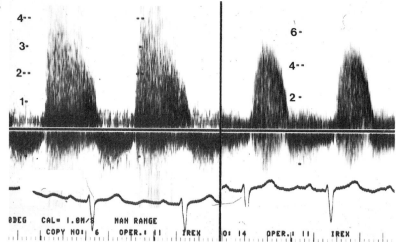

152 Doppler echocardiogram (continuous wave). On the right, the high velocity (5 M/s) of left ventricular ejection can be seen reflecting severe aortic stenosis. On the left, aortic regurgitation is seen taken from an apical view.

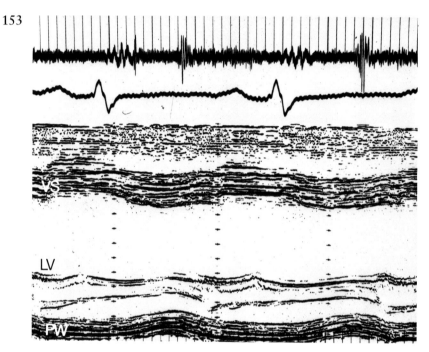

153 M-mode echocardiogram through the left ventricle. In aortic regurgitation associated with heart failure, the left ventricular cavity is often enlarged, but its function may or may not be preserved. In this example, there is gross left ventricular dilatation with poor contraction of the left ventricle (LV). PW – posterior wall; VS – ventricular septum.

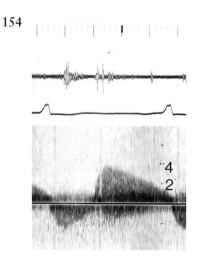

154 Continuous wave Doppler (apical view). The severity of aortic regurgitation by Doppler is shown by the low aortic left ventricular gradient at end-diastole reflecting a high left ventricular end-diastolic pressure.

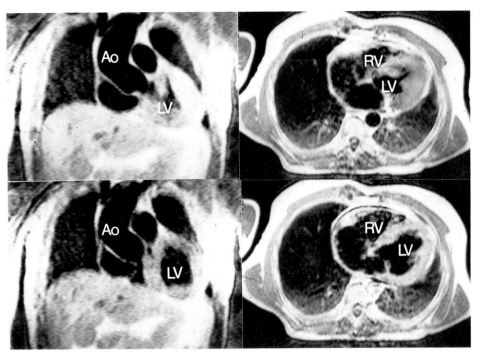

155 Magnetic resonance scan (systole above, diastole below; coronal sections on the left, transverse sections on the right) in aortic stenosis showing severe left ventricular hypertrophy. Ao – aorta; LV – left ventricle; RV – right ventricle.

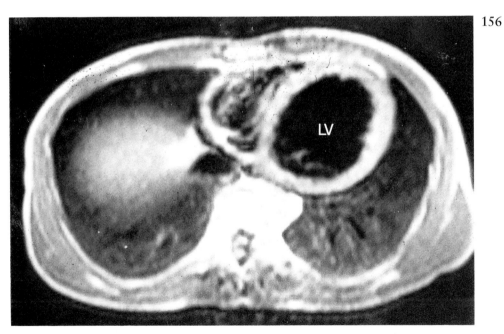

156 Magnetic resonance scan (saggital section) in aortic regurgitation showing a grossly dilated left ventricle (LV).

157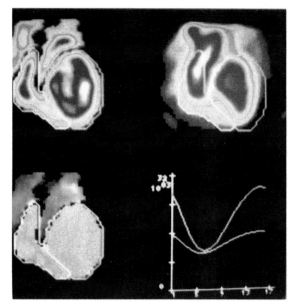

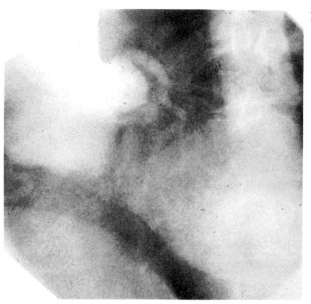 **158**

157 Gated blood pool scan in aortic regurgitation showing a dilated left ventricle (end-diastolic image, top right). The amplitude image (top left) shows a basal defect typical of aortic regurgitation with a normal phase image (bottom left). Left ventricular (blue) and right ventricular (yellow) volume time curves showing a left ventricular ejection fraction of 58% and a right ventricular ejection fraction of 35%; left ventricular stroke volume/right ventricular stroke volume = 2.3 (bottom right).

158 Aortogram (left anterior oblique projection) in aortic regurgitation showing moderate regurgitation across the aortic valve. The valve is bicuspid.

159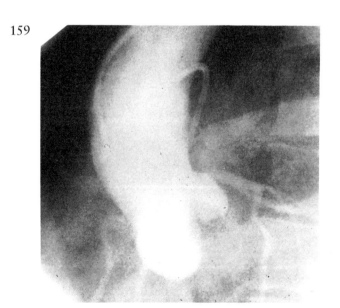

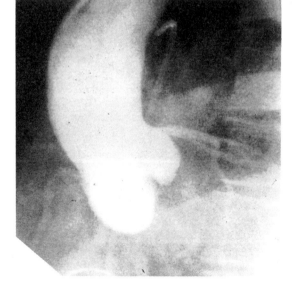

159 & 160 Aortogram (left anterior oblique projection; systole **159**, diastole **160**) in aortic stenosis showing that the valve barely opens.

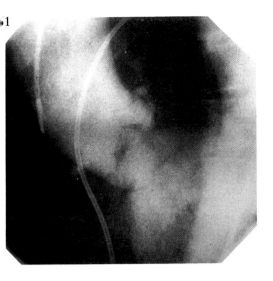
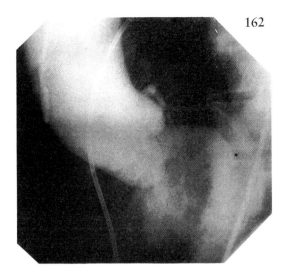

161 & 162 Aortogram (left anterior oblique projection; systole **161**, diastole **162**) showing severe aortic regurgitation with the left ventricle filled from the aortogram. The aortic root is dilated and the aortic valve is bicuspid.

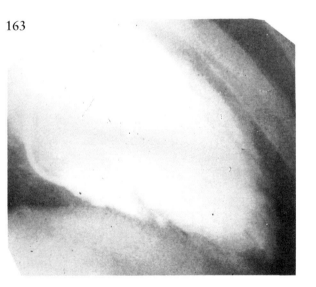
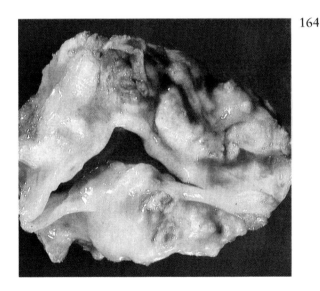

163 Left ventriculogram (right anterior oblique projection) showing an end-systolic frame in aortic regurgitation and heart failure. The left ventricular cavity is dilated.

164 Macroscopic section of an excised degenerative aortic valve in aortic stenosis.

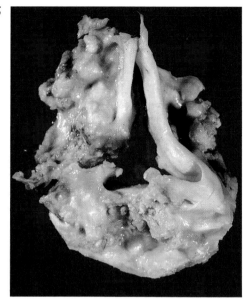

165 Excised tricuspid aortic valve which has undergone severe degeneration. Each of the three cusps is heavily calcified and immobile. The orifice is severely stenotic.

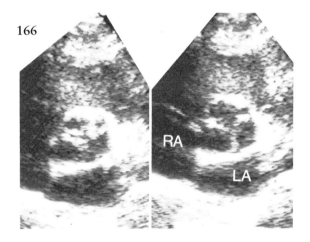

166 Cross sectional echocardiogram (parasternal short axis view) shows in diastole (right) that the aortic valve is tricuspid and in systole (left) opens to a slit-like orifice. LA – left atrium; RA – right atrium.

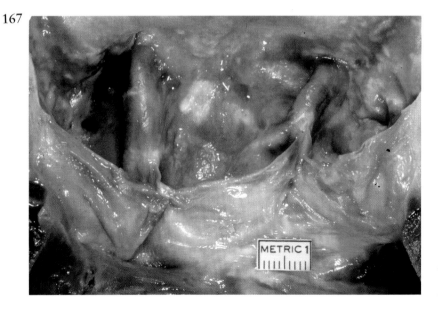

167 Macroscopic view of the aortic sinuses of a 66-year-old man with Marfan's syndrome. The sinuses are large, bulging and prolapse outwards.

168 Photomicrographs of a normal ascending aorta (left) and aorta from a man with Marfan's syndrome (right). There is considerable loss of elastic fibres (stained black) in the Marfan aorta and increased mucoid material (stained green).

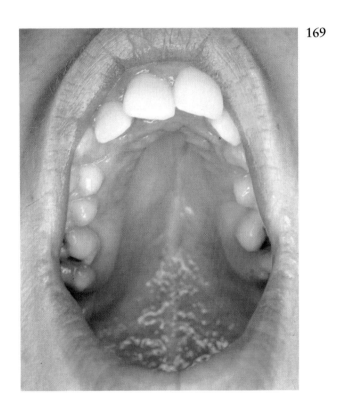

169

169 High arch palate in Marfan's syndrome.

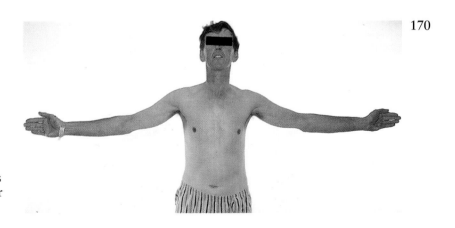

170

170 Classically, patients with Marfan's syndrome have long arms and the span of their arms is greater than their height.

171

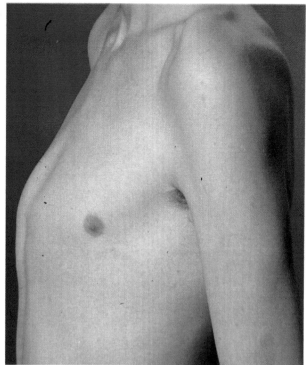

171 Chest deformity (pectus excavatus) is common in Marfan's syndrome.

172

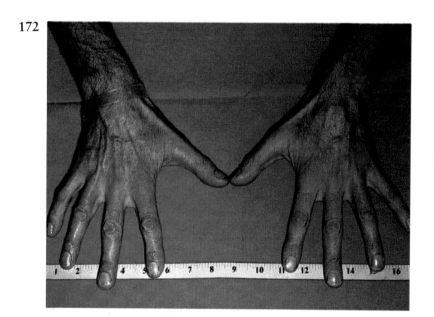

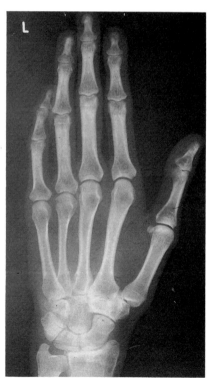

1

172 & 173 Patients with Marfan's syndrome have fingers that are long and spindly (arachnodactyly) (**172**) which can be objectively assessed by measuring the metacarpal index (**173**).
Arachnodactyly is a classical but not pathognomonic feature of Marfan's syndrome.

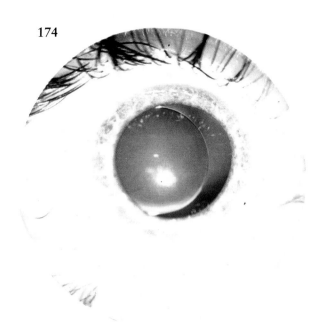

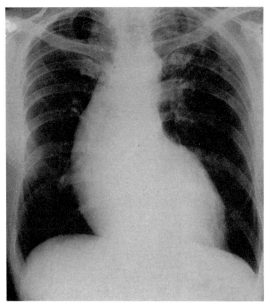

174 In Marfan's syndrome posterior dislocation of the lens may occur.

175 Chest radiograph in Marfan's syndrome with aortic regurgitation showing gross dilatation of the aorta. There is early pulmonary venous congestion.

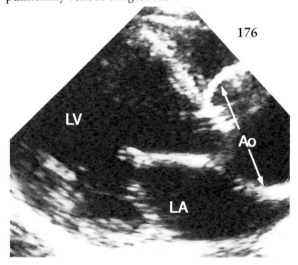

176

176 Cross sectional echocardiogram (parasternal long axis view). The aortic root dilatation in Marfan's syndrome may readily be demonstrated by cross sectional echocardiography. In this example, the aortic root (arrows) is more than 6 cm in diameter which is twice the normal measurement. LA – left atrium; LV – left ventricle.

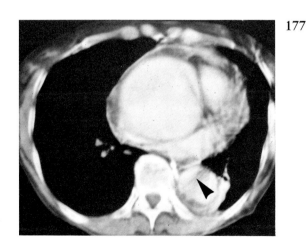

177

177 Computed tomography showing a grossly dilated ascending aorta in Marfan's syndrome. There is, in addition, a dissection flap (arrow) in the descending aorta.

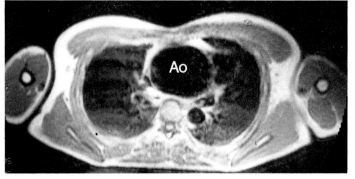

178 Magnetic resonance scan. In the saggital section the gross dilatation of the ascending aorta (Ao) is seen in Marfan's syndrome.

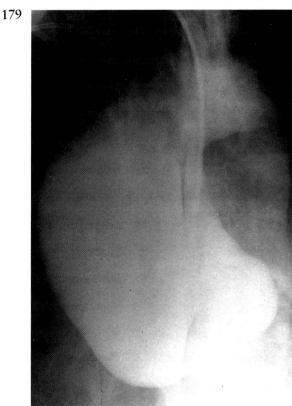

179 Aortogram (left anterior oblique projection) showing a massively dilated ascending aorta with aortic regurgitation in Marfan's syndrome.

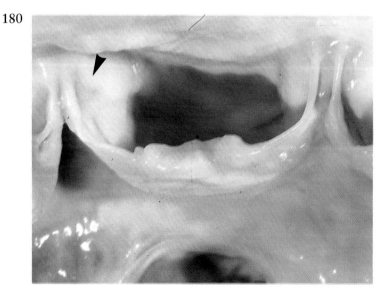

180 Aortic valve in ankylosing spondylitis with aortic regurgitation showing inflammation and thickening behind and immediately above the sinus of Valsalva; this is particularly dense behind and adjacent to the aortic valve commisures (arrow). The valve cusps are shortened and slightly thickened.

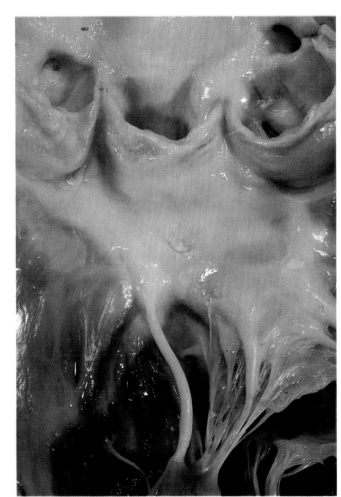

181 Aortic valve and adjacent anterior mitral valve leaflet in ankylosing spondylitis. Dense advential scar is present adjacent to the aortic valve commisures and extends below the base of the valve producing a subvalvular ridge. This fibrous tissue also extends into the base of the anterior mitral valve leaflet. The aortic cusps are shortened and diffusely thickened.

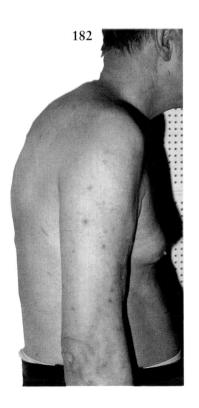

182

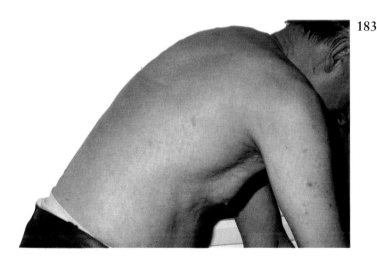

183

182 & 183 Clinical photograph showing loss of normal spinal curvature (**182**) with limited flexion (**183**) in ankylosing spondylitis.

184

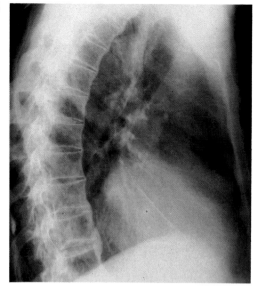

184 Thoracic spinal radiograph in ankylosing spondylitis.

185

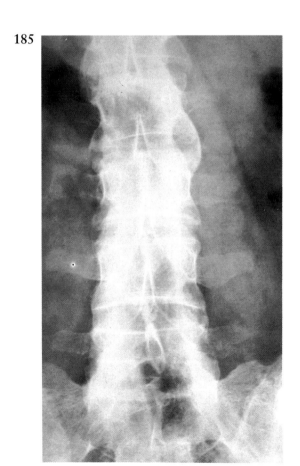

18

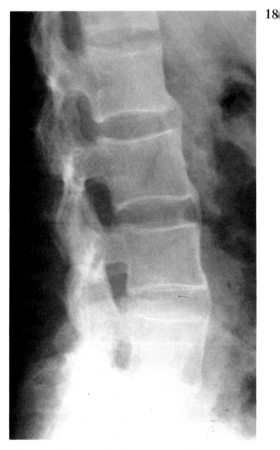

185 & 186 X-rays of the spine (postero-anterior view **185**, lateral view **186**) in ankylosing spondylitis showing ossification of the ligaments of the spine.

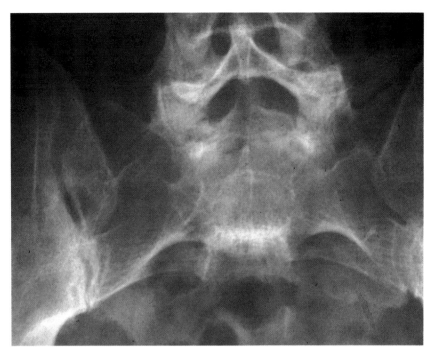

187 Pelvic radiograph in a patient with ankylosing spondylitis showing loss of joint space and fusion of the sacro-iliac joints.

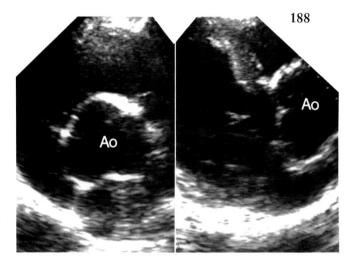

188 Cross sectional echocardiogram (parasternal short axis view right; long axis view left). This shows dilatation of the aortic root (Ao) in ankylosing spondylitis.

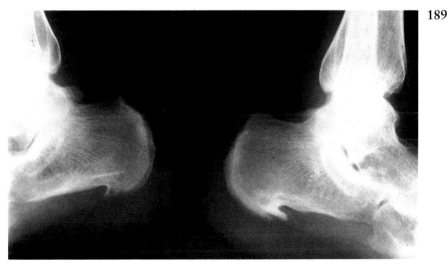

189 Heel radiograph showing plantar spurs which is a characteristic feature of Reiter's syndrome.

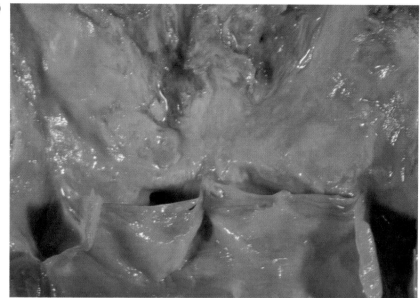

190 Macroscopic section showing the ascending aorta of an elderly man with syphilis. The aorta is extremely dilated above the sino-tubular junction and there is extensive atherosclerotic plaque.

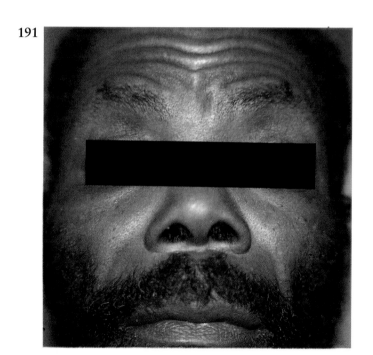

191 Facial appearance in a patient with tabes dorsalis.

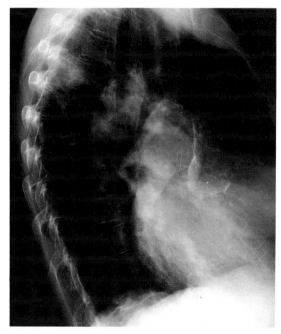

192 Chest radiograph (lateral projection) showing calcification of the ascending aorta in syphilitic aortitis.

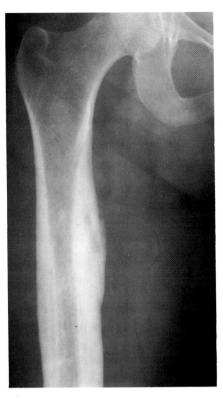

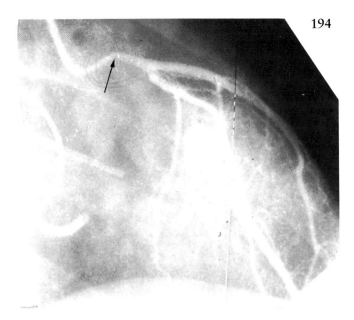

194 Coronary arteriogram (right anterior oblique projection). This shows the characteristic features of syphilitic aortitis with ostial stenosis of the left coronary artery (arrow).

193 Radiograph of the femur showing a gumma.

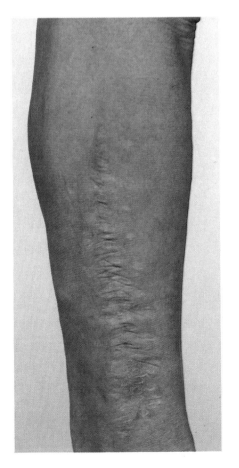

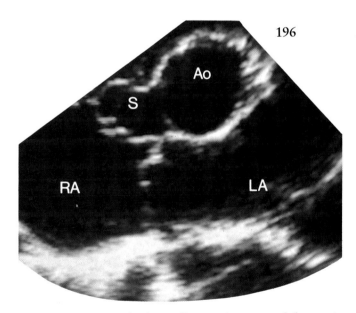

196 Cross sectional echocardiogram (parasternal short axis view). Ruptured sinus of Valsalva aneurysm may present with features similar to aortic regurgitation and heart failure. In this example, a ruptured sinus of Valsalva (S) into the right ventricle can be seen to the right of the aortic root. Ao – aorta; LA – left atrium; RA – right atrium.

195 Clinical photograph in the Ehlers Danlos syndrome showing abnormal scarring of the leg. Many connective tissue diseases are associated with aortic regurgitation.

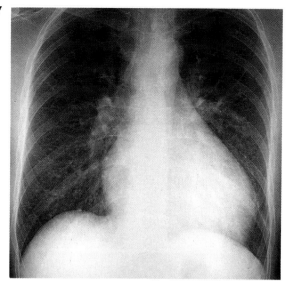

197 Chest radiograph in ruptured sinus of Valsalva aneurysm. There is cardiomegaly and pulmonary plethora.

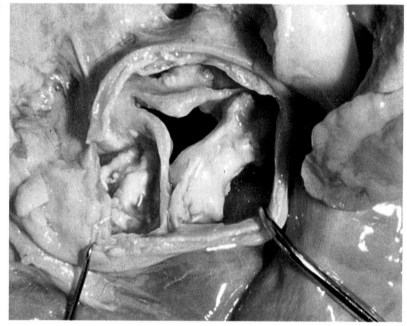

198 Macroscopic section showing a rheumatic tricuspid aortic valve that is stenosed.

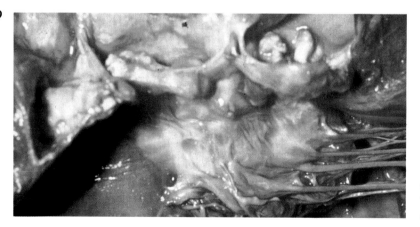

199 Macroscopic section through the aortic valve with the heart opened showing a rheumatic tricuspid stenosed and regurgitant aortic valve.

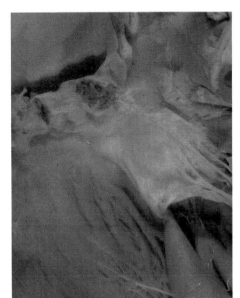

200 Macroscopic section showing the left ventricle in rheumatic aortic regurgitation. The left ventricle is hypertrophied and dilated.

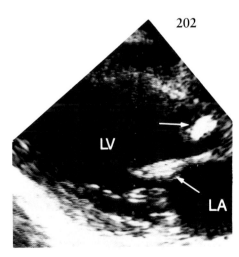

201 Chest radiograph (lateral projection) showing mixed rheumatic aortic and mitral valve disease, both valves are calcified.

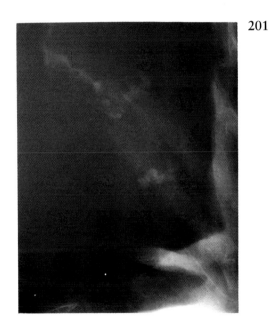

202 Cross sectional echocardiogram (parasternal long axis view). There is rheumatic involvement of both the aortic and mitral valves with calcification and degeneration (arrows). LA – left atrium; LV – left ventricle.

Chronic mitral valve disease

The commonest causes of chronic mitral valve disease are rheumatic heart disease and floppy mitral valve. Rheumatic heart disease will cause mitral stenosis and mitral regurgitation although dominant mitral regurgitation is usually non-rheumatic and most often due to a floppy mitral valve. Mitral stenosis will usually cause a low output state and heart failure in the presence of a small heart with left atrial enlargement. The development of shortness of breath and heart failure is often insidious and the diagnosis is most easily made using cross sectional echocardiography in which specific features of rheumatic mitral valve disease are evident.

Floppy mitral valve is a very common finding and usually causes no symptoms. Only when it is severe and particularly in the presence of ruptured chordae will it lead to heart failure. The development of ruptured chordae may present acutely (see earlier section) or with the progressive breathlessness and heart failure. Again the diagnosis is best made using echocardiography, but angiography is required to assess the severity of the regurgitation.

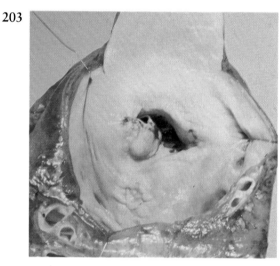

203 Macroscopic section showing a thick mitral valve viewed from the left atrium. The valve is severely stenosed and the left atrium is enlarged.

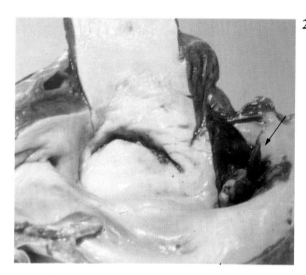

204 Mitral stenosis showing left atrial appendage thrombus (arrow).

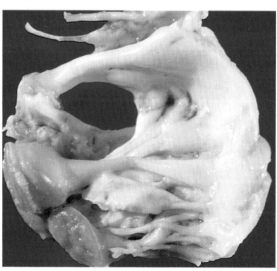

205 Excised mitral valve viewed from the side showing thickening of subvalvular apparatus in rheumatic mitral stenosis.

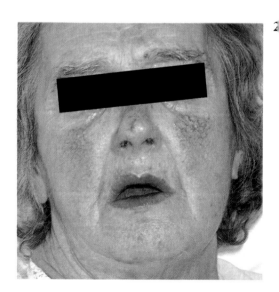

206 Typical malar flush of mitral stenosis. This is a non-specific finding due to a low cardiac output.

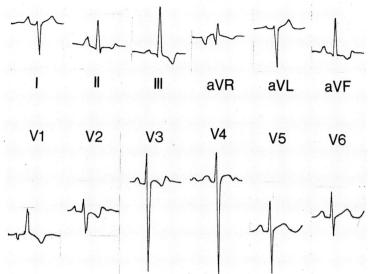

207 Electrocardiogram in severe mitral stenosis showing right ventricular hypertrophy due to the development of pulmonary hypertension. Left atrial enlargement is also present.

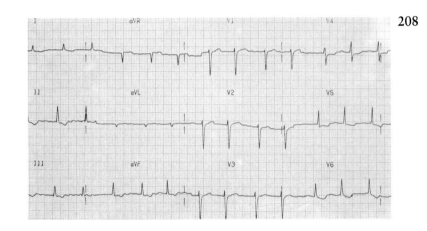

208 Electrocardiogram in mitral stenosis frequently shows atrial fibrillation. The effects of Digoxin are also evident.

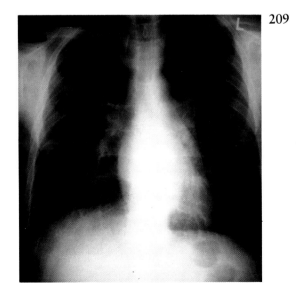

209 Chest radiograph in mitral stenosis showing an enlarged left atrium and appendage without overall enlargement of the cardiac silhouette. On this penetrated film, the pulmonary venous congestion is not clearly seen.

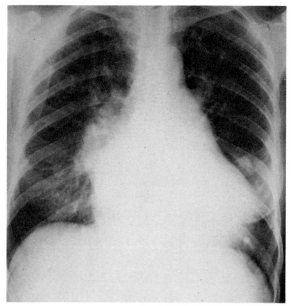

210 Chest radiograph in mitral stenosis and regurgitation with heart failure. There is pulmonary oedema and the heart size is enlarged.

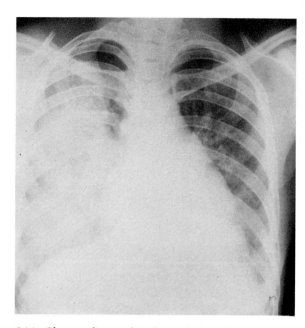

211 Chest radiograph in heart failure due to mitral stenosis. In this example, in contrast to **210**, the pulmonary oedema is unilateral. This is a rare, but well known phenomena.

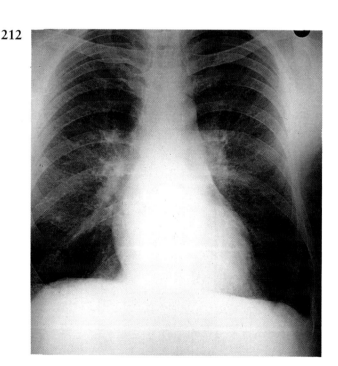
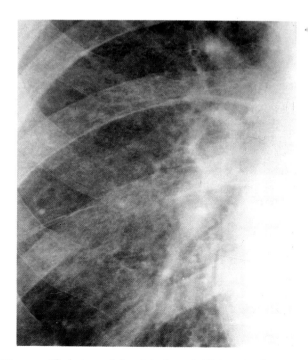

212 & 213 Chest radiograph (postero-anterior projection **212**, magnified view of the right lung **213**) in mitral stenosis showing haemosiderosis. This reticular nodular shadowing is related to chronic pulmonary oedema.

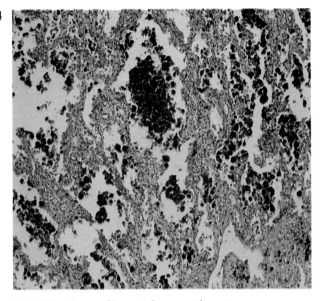

214 Histology of lung in haemosiderosis.

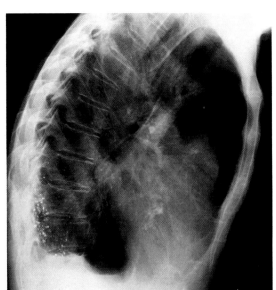

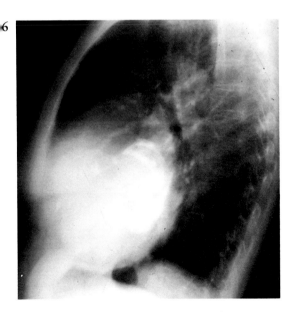

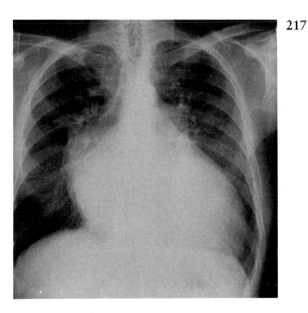

215 & 216 Chest radiographs (lateral projection) showing calcification in the mitral valve (215) and calcified thrombus in the left atrium (216).

217 Chest radiograph in rheumatic mitral regurgitation. The heart is enlarged and there is left atrial enlargement with pulmonary venous congestion.

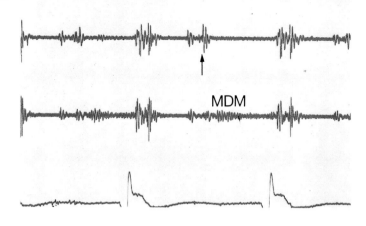

218 Phonocardiogram in mitral stenosis showing an opening snap (arrow) and mid-diastolic murmur (MDM).

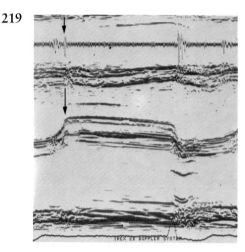

219 M-mode echocardiogram. The thickening of the mitral valve is seen with tethering of the anterior and posterior leaflets. This produces a characteristic appearance. The timing of the opening snap (arrow) can be seen and related to the cessation of rapid anterior motion of the anterior mitral valve in diastole.

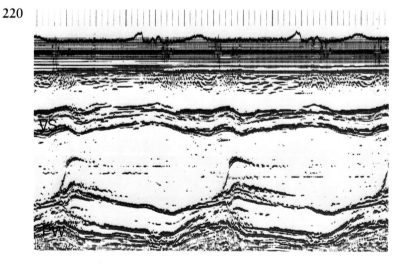

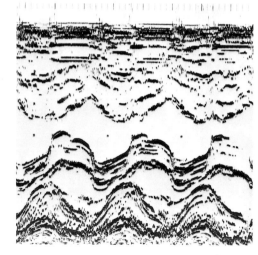

220 M-mode echocardiogram. The characteristic haemodynamic feature of mitral stenosis is slow left ventricular filling. In this echocardiogram the slow posterior motion of the posterior wall (PW) and abnormal septal motion (VS) can be seen.

221 M-mode echocardiogram. The association of mitral stenosis and regurgitation gives the feature of a rheumatic stenotic valve by M-mode echocardiography and rapid left ventricular filling reflecting the severity of mitral regurgitation.

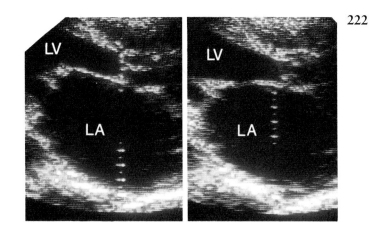

222

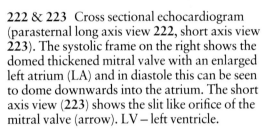

222 & 223 Cross sectional echocardiogram (parasternal long axis view **222**, short axis view **223**). The systolic frame on the right shows the domed thickened mitral valve with an enlarged left atrium (LA) and in diastole this can be seen to dome downwards into the atrium. The short axis view (**223**) shows the slit like orifice of the mitral valve (arrow). LV – left ventricle.

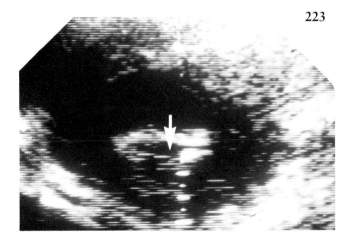

223

224 Cross sectional echocardiogram (parasternal long axis view right, short axis view left). The calcification of the valve starts initially on the valve free margin and this can be seen in both the long and short axis view. With calcification, evaluation of orifice size of a rheumatic valve becomes difficult. LA – left atrium.

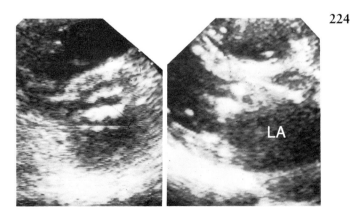

224

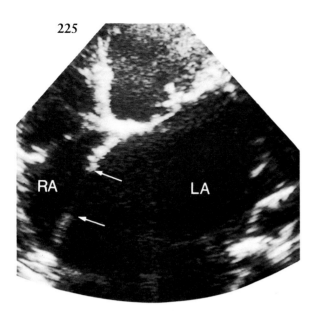

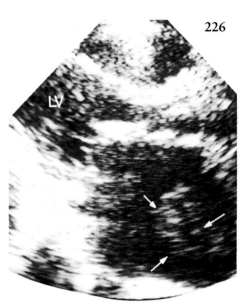

225 Cross sectional echocardiogram (apical long axis view). Gross enlargement of the left atrium (LA) may occur in rheumatic mitral valve disease as in this example. It may be noted that the interatrial septum (arrows) bulges into the right atrium (RA) reflecting left atrial pressure.

226 Cross sectional echocardiogram (parasternal long axis view). There is a rounded thrombus in the left atrium (arrows). In real time imaging, this mass can be seen to be mobile. This is a common complication of mitral stenosis with atrial fibrillation. LV – left ventricle.

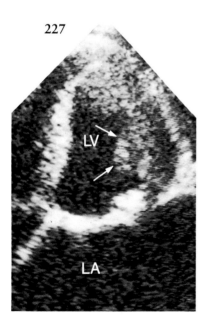

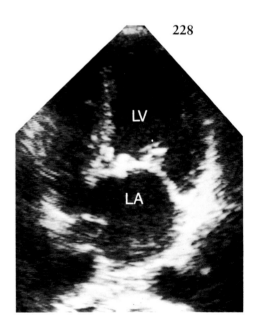

227 Cross sectional echocardiogram (apical long axis view). A clot may occur in the left ventricle (LV) as well as that in the left atrium (LA) (arrows).

228 Cross sectional echocardiogram (apical long axis view). While most cases of mitral stenosis are rheumatic in origin, occasionally they are congenitally caused. The valve has a similar appearance by echocardiography although it is not domed and tethered in the same way. LA – left atrium; LV – left ventricle.

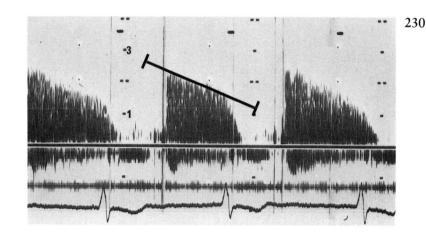

229 Continuous wave Doppler echocardiogram (apical view). In this example, the peak velocity of transmitral flow is 2.5 M/s which is almost twice the normal value and there is a slow decline (prolonged pressure half time). As the patient is in sinus rhythm, the atrial peak (A) can be seen.

230 Continuous wave Doppler echocardiogram (apical view). With the loss of atrial systole the atrial peak can no longer be seen, but the severity of mitral stenosis can be assessed by the rate of decline (slope) of the peak velocity across the mitral valve.

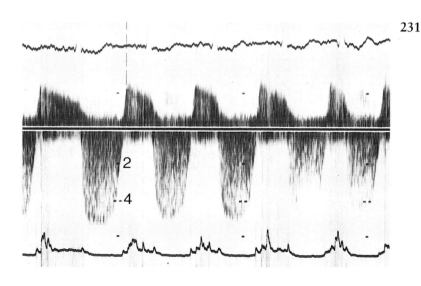

231 Continuous wave Doppler echocardiogram (apical view). In mixed mitral stenosis and regurgitation both the reduction in the decline of peak velocity across the mitral valve may be seen as well as the regurgitant jet.

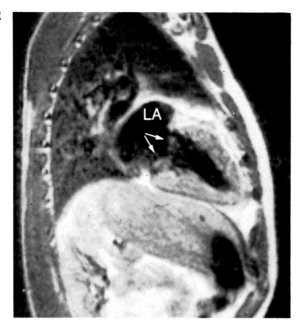

232 Magnetic resonance scan (saggital section) showing a thickened mitral valve (arrows) and enlarged left atrium (LA).

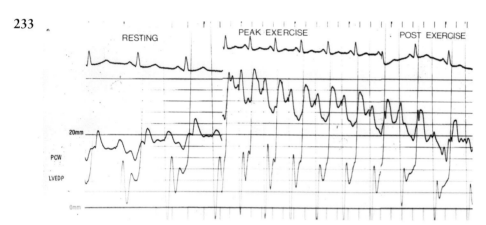

233 Haemodynamic trace in mitral stenosis showing a small gradient between the pulmonary capillary wedge pressure and the left ventricular end-diastolic pressure due to the mitral stenosis; with exercise this gradient increases markedly and recovers after exercise.

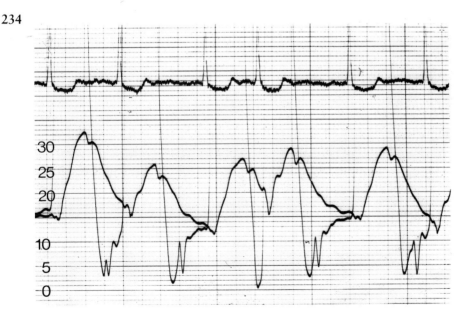

234 Haemodynamic trace in mitral stenosis and regurgitation showing dominant mitral regurgitation which is evident by a tall systolic wave in the pulmonary capillary wedge pressure trace and there is only a small gradient across the mitral valve evident on the shorter R-R intervals.

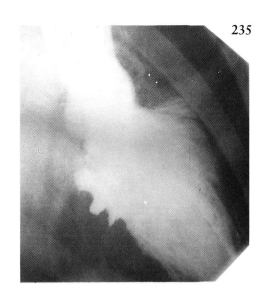

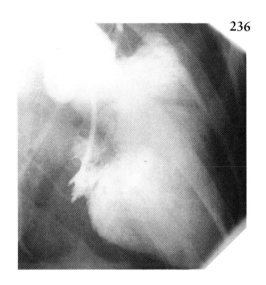

235 & 236 Left ventricular angiogram (systole **235**, diastole **236**) in mitral stenosis showing a small left ventricular cavity without mitral regurgitation. The valve is deformed.

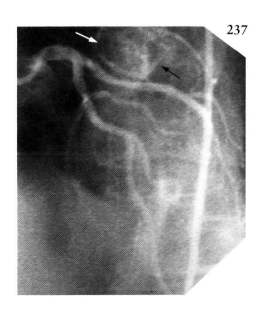

237 Left coronary arteriogram (left anterior oblique projection) showing neovascularisation of a clot in the left atrium (arrows) filling from the left circumflex.

238

239

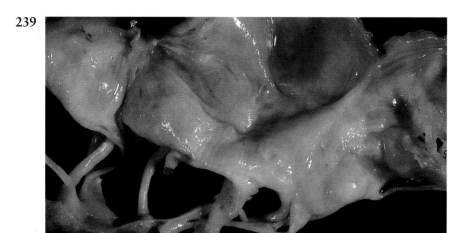

238 & 239 Macroscopic sections showing a floppy mitral valve with ruptured chordae tendinae (238). There is increased surface area of the valve leaflets producing a scalloped appearance with focal fibrous thickening of the leaflets and the chordae tendinae. These features are also evident on the excised valve prior to surgery (239).

240

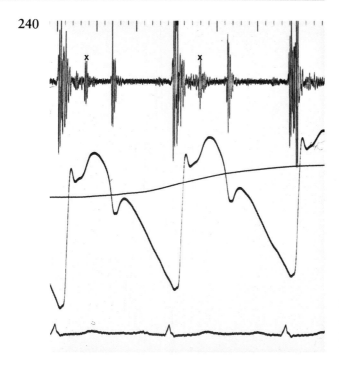

240 Phonocardiogram and carotid pulse in mitral valve prolapse (x) showing a systolic click.

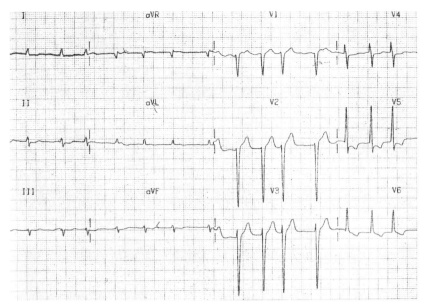

241 Electrocardiogram in mitral regurgitation due to floppy mitral valve showing atrial fibrillation with left ventricular hypertrophy and left axis deviation.

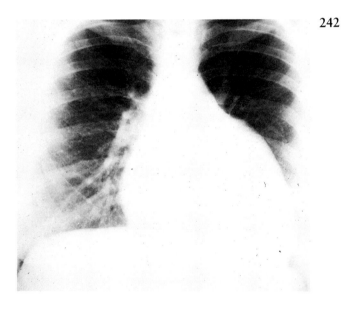

242 Chest radiograph (postero-anterior projection) in mitral regurgitation due to floppy valve showing an enlarged heart with pulmonary congestion. The left atrium is also enlarged.

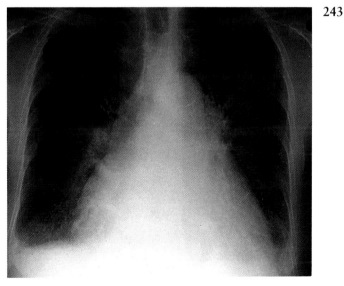

243 Chest radiograph (postero-anterior projection) in ruptured chordae secondary to a floppy mitral valve. This patient was in severe heart failure and the radiograph shows an enlarged heart with heart failure.

244

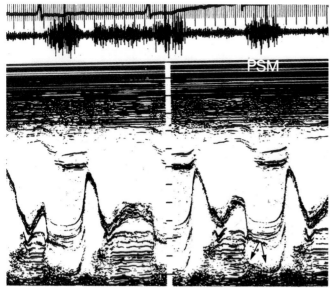

244 M-mode echocardiogram. Mild mitral valve prolapse is not associated with heart failure. Severe mitral prolapse associated with haemodynamically significant mitral regurgitation is seen in this example. There are multiple echoes in diastole and holosystolic prolapse (arrows) of the mitral valve is seen concomitantly with the pansystolic murmur (PSM).

245

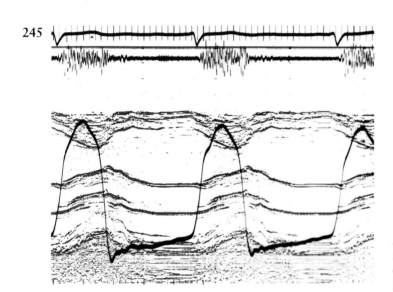

245 M-mode echocardiogram. Severe mitral regurgitation of non-rheumatic origin. In this example, the left ventricle is dilated but has moderately good contraction.

246

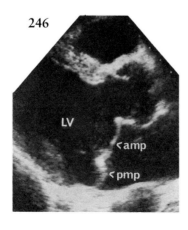

246 Cross sectional echocardiogram (parasternal long axis view). Prolapse of both the anterior (amp) and posterior (pmp) mitral valve leaflets can be seen as well as mild dilatation of the mitral valve ring and left atrium.

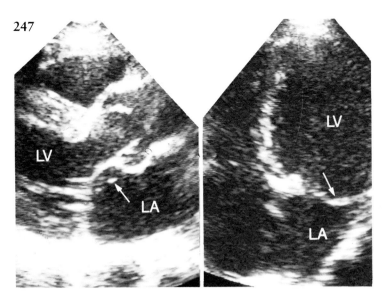

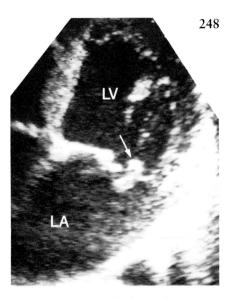

247 Cross sectional echocardiogram (parasternal long axis view left, apical long axis view right). In this case of a floppy mitral valve, ruptured chordae (arrow) can be seen prolapsing into the left atrium (LA) in these systolic frames. Ruptured chordae in this patient was associated with the onset of severe mitral regurgitation and heart failure. LV – left ventricle.

248 Cross sectional echocardiogram (apical long axis view). Chronic ruptured chordae become thickened and fibrotic and can be seen here as masses attached to the mitral valve (arrows). LA – left atrium; LV – left ventricle.

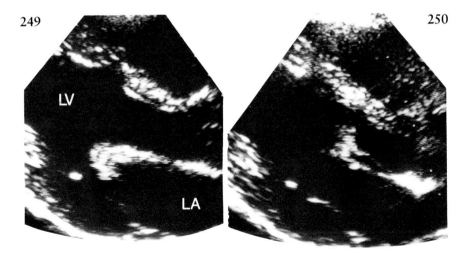

249 & 250 Cross sectional echocardiogram (parasternal long axis view; systole **249**, diastole **250**). Mitral valve prolapse may become very severe with marked reduplication of the valve leaflets associated with regurgitation. In this example, the valve appears very thick and long and prolapses into the left atrium (LA) in systole and across the left ventricular outflow tract in diastole. LV – left ventricle.

251

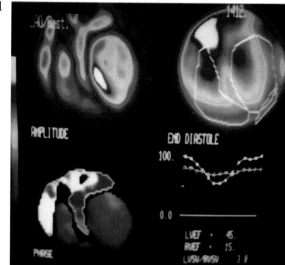

251 Gated blood pool scan showing a dilated left ventricle in mitral regurgitation (end-diastolic image, top right). The amplitude image shows hypokinesis of the anterolateral wall (top left) with a normal phase image (bottom left). The left ventricular and right ventricular volume time curves (bottom right) show a left ventricular ejection fraction of 45% and right ventricular ejection fraction of 15%; left ventricular stroke volume/right ventricular stroke volume = 3.8.

252

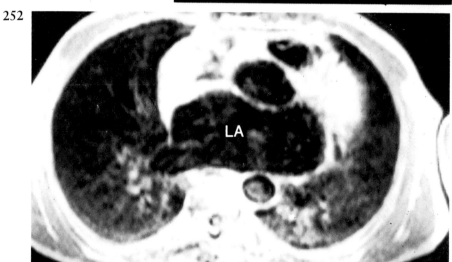

252 Magnetic resonance scan (saggital section) in mitral valve prolapse showing a large left atrium (LA).

253

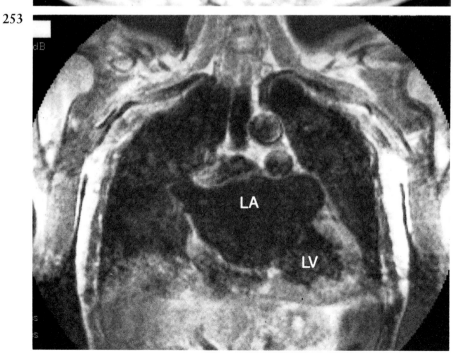

253 Magnetic resonance scan (coronal section) in severe mitral regurgitation showing a dilated left ventricle (LV) and left atrium (LA).

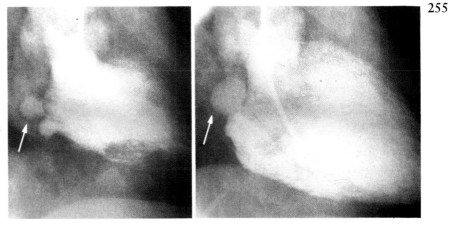

254 Haemodynamic tracing showing the pulmonary capillary wedge pressure (pcw) and left ventricular end-diastolic pressure in severe mitral regurgitation secondary to a floppy mitral valve. The V wave exceeds 50 mmHg. There is no gradient across the mitral valve.

255 Left ventricular angiogram (systole left, diastole right) showing a floppy mitral valve with filling of the left atrium due to mitral regurgitation. The floppy mitral valve is clearly seen as a collection of contrast within the mitral valve prolapsing into the left atrium (arrowed).

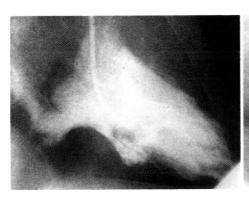

256 Left ventricular angiogram (systole left, diastole right) in mitral regurgitation with heart failure. There is severe mitral regurgitation through a localised jet and a floppy valve. The left ventricle is dilated.

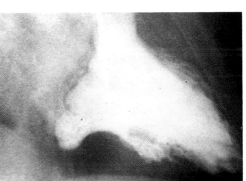

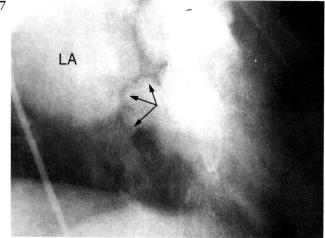

257 Left ventricular angiogram showing gross mitral regurgitation through a floppy valve (arrows) as dense opacification of the left atrium (LA). This caused severe heart failure.

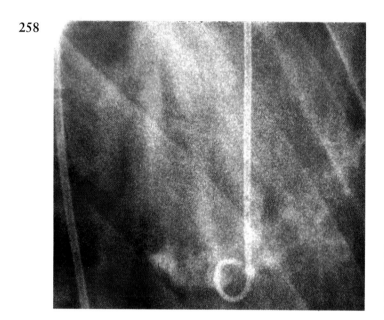

258 Fluoroscopy of the mitral valve ring showing annular calcification in non-rheumatic mitral regurgitation. This patient was also in heart failure.

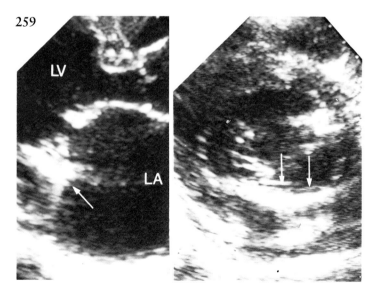

259 Cross sectional echocardiogram (parasternal long axis view left, short axis view right). Calcification of the posterior aspect of the mitral valve annulus can be seen (arrows). The mitral valve itself is calcified and immobile and the annular calcification has lead to haemodynamically significant mitral stenosis and heart failure. LA – left atrium; LV – left ventricle.

Tricuspid valve disease

Isolated tricuspid valve disease will cause right heart failure. Isolated involvement of the tricuspid valve is rare, but does occur in certain specific circumstances such as endocarditis in drug addicts, tricuspid valve prolapse, carcinoid syndrome and Ebstein's anomaly.

Most frequently, tricuspid regurgitation is secondary to rheumatic mitral valve disease and biventricular failure is often present. Very rarely, the rheumatic process can also involve the tricuspid valve causing tricuspid stenosis. Again, in the presence of mitral valve disease, there will be biventricular failure.

Disease of the tricuspid valve, particularly tricuspid stenosis, is often missed clinically. The non-invasive investigation of choice is cross sectional echocardiography together with Doppler which allows assessment of the gradient. Haemodynamics and angiography are usually unhelpful.

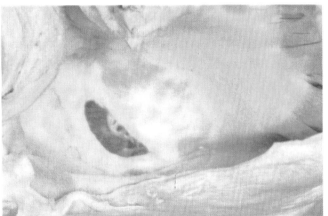 **260**

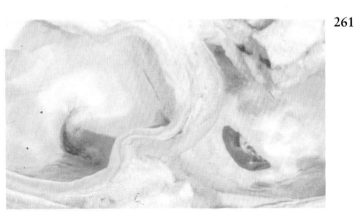 **261**

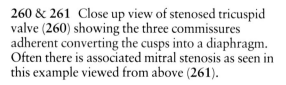 **260 & 261** Close up view of stenosed tricuspid valve (**260**) showing the three commissures adherent converting the cusps into a diaphragm. Often there is associated mitral stenosis as seen in this example viewed from above (**261**).

262

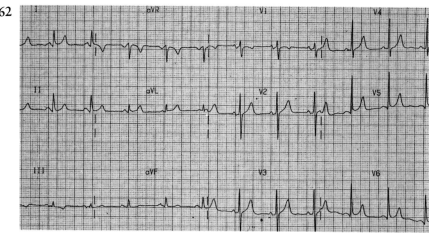

263

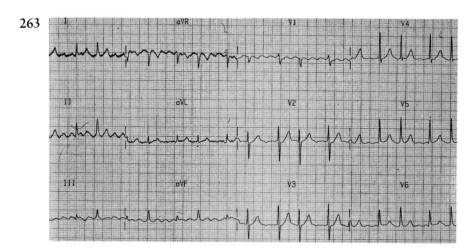

262 & 263 Electrocardiogram in rheumatic mitral and tricuspid stenosis. There is atrial enlargement when the patient is in sinus rhythm (**262**). Subsequently, the patient developed atrial fibrillation (**263**).

264

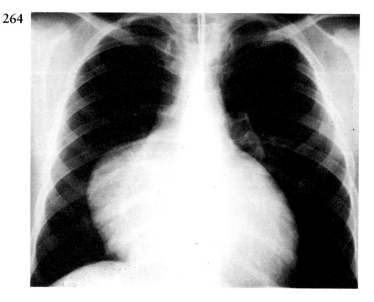

264 Chest radiograph (postero-anterior projection) in a young patient with isolated tricuspid regurgitation showing a grossly enlarged right atrium.

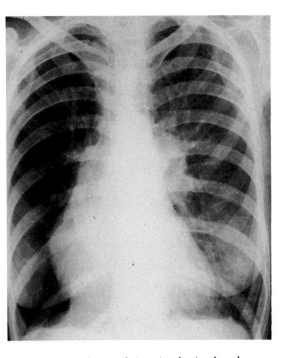

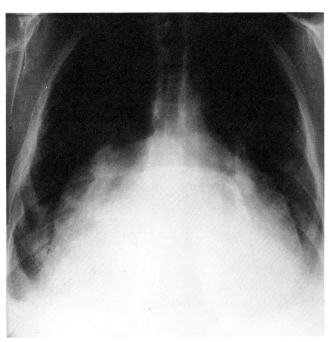

265 Chest radiograph in mixed mitral and tricuspid stenosis. There is evidence of both left and right atrial enlargement, with upper lobe blood diversion.

266 Chest radiograph (postero-anterior projection) in mixed mitral valve disease with secondary tricuspid regurgitation showing gross cardiomegaly involving the right atrium.

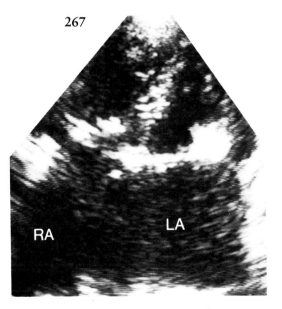

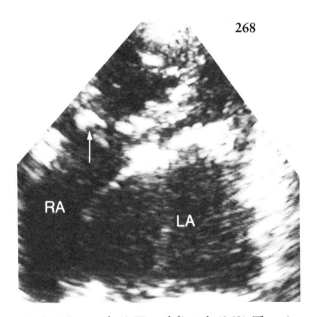

267 & 268 Cross sectional echocardiogram (apical long axis view) in systole (**267**) and diastole (**268**). There is rheumatic and tricuspid stenosis. The thickened tricuspid valve (arrow) can be seen to dome in diastole. LA – left atrium; RA – right atrium.

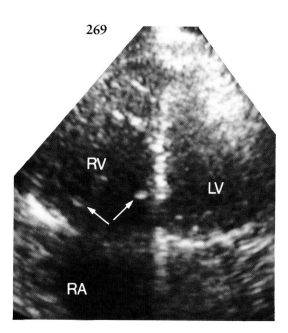

269

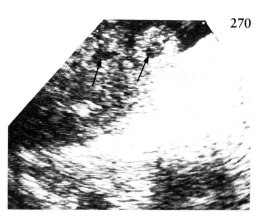

270

270 Liver ultrasound. Multiple filling defects (arrows) are seen in a patient with carcinoid syndrome.

269 Cross sectional echocardiogram (apical long axis view). Carcinoid involvement of the tricuspid valve produces a typical appearance as in this case with thickening of the valve cusps in the half open position (arrows). LV – left ventricle; RA – right atrium; RV – right ventricle.

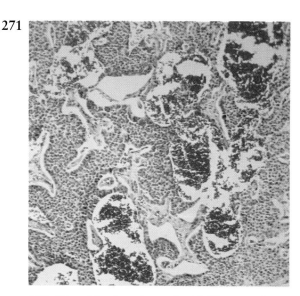

271

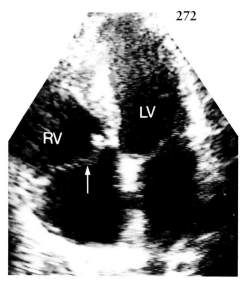

272

271 Liver histology in carcinoid. There are large blood filled sinusoids.

272 Cross sectional echocardiogram (parasternal long axis view). Tricuspid valve prolapse (arrow) is frequently associated with mitral valve prolapse and may be a cause of tricuspid regurgitation. LV – left ventricle; RV – right ventricle.

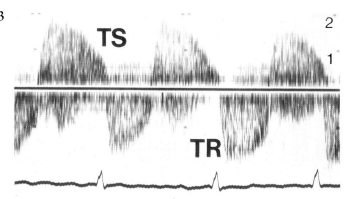

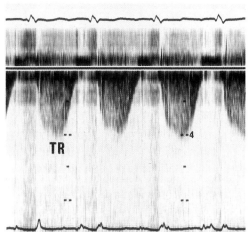

273 Continuous wave Doppler echocardiogram (parasternal view). Doppler ultrasound is probably the method of choice for detecting and quantifying tricuspid stenosis. In addition, this patient has mild tricuspid regurgitation.

274 Continuous wave Doppler (parasternal view). In pulmonary hypertension with tricuspid regurgitation, the peak velocity of the tricuspid regurgitant jet is equal to the right ventricular systolic pressure. In this example, the peak velocity is 4 M/s which equates to a right ventricular systolic pressure of approximately 64 mmHg.

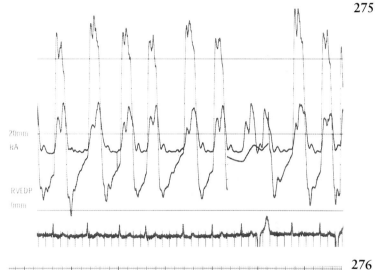

275 Haemodynamic tracing in tricuspid stenosis showing a gradient across the tricuspid valve. There is a tall V wave indicating tricuspid regurgitation.

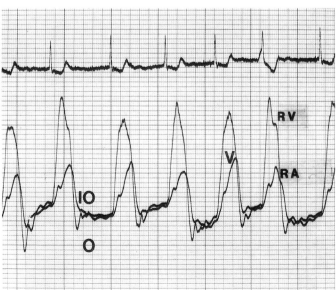

276 Haemodynamic tracing in tricuspid regurgitation showing a tall V wave in the right atrial pressure trace; there is no gradient across the tricuspid valve.

Valve surgery

Valve surgery can lead to heart failure for a number of reasons. If the operation is delayed such that left ventricular function is already severely impaired, particularly in aortic or mitral regurgitation, then heart failure will develop post-operatively.

Mechanical valves may become regurgitant particularly around the seating of the valves. Rarely, they may be stenosed due to thrombosis and tissue ingrowth.

Following mitral valvotomy, restenosis may occur at varying intervals up to several decades. Mitral regurgitation following mitral valvotomy is an early phenomenon and is rarely seen after the initial stages. Mitral valve repair may be the method of choice for treating the floppy mitral valve but occasionally may not be effective or may even lead to mitral stenosis.

Bioprosthetic valves tend to degenerate after about 7-10 years usually causing valvular regurgitation but there may also be associated stenosis. The rate of degeneration of the different bioprosthetic valves varies.

Endocarditis is an important complication following valve replacement, usually leading to regurgitation and often requiring re-operation.

277

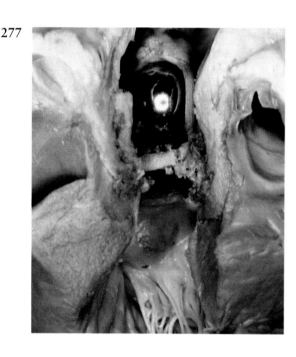

277 Macroscopic view of an aortic Starr-Edwards valve *in situ*.

278

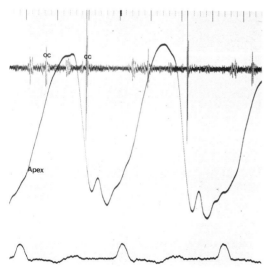

278 Phonocardiogram and apex cardiogram showing opening (oc) and closing clicks (cc) of an aortic Starr-Edwards valve in a patient with heart failure due to poor left ventricular function as evidenced by the slow rising and sustained impulse of the apex cardiogram.

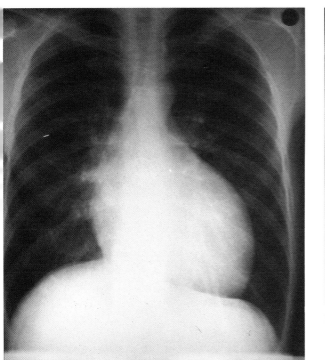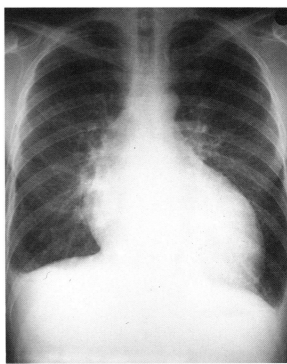

279 & 280 Chest radiographs immediately following an aortic valve replacement for aortic regurgitation (**279**). Initially, the valve was competent but subsequently developed aortic regurgitation and left ventricular failure (**280**).

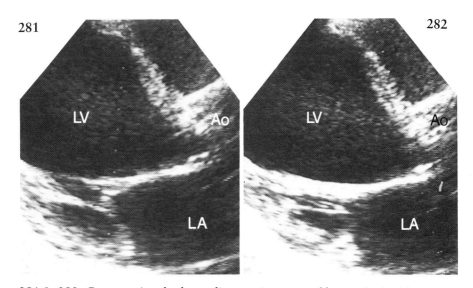

281 & 282 Cross sectional echocardiogram (parasternal long axis view) in systole (**281**), diastole (**282**). This patient has a dilated left ventricle (LV) which contracts poorly. The echoes within the aortic root (Ao) represent the Starr-Edwards aortic valve replacement. LA – left atrium.

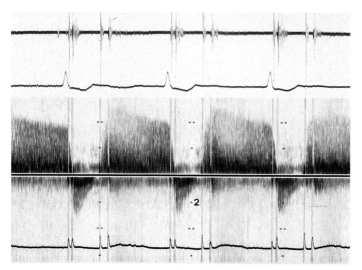

283 Continuous wave Doppler echocardiogram (apical view). Doppler echocardiography may detect the presence of aortic regurgitation in prosthetic valves. The timing of the regurgitation may be seen in relationship to the valve opening and closing.

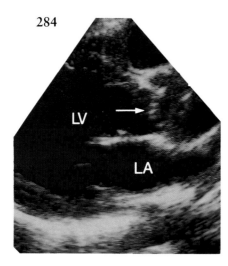

284 Cross sectional echocardiogram (parasternal long axis view). Degeneration of aortic valve homografts may appear as prolapse of one or more of the valvular cusps as seen in this example (arrow). LA – left atrium; LV – left ventricle.

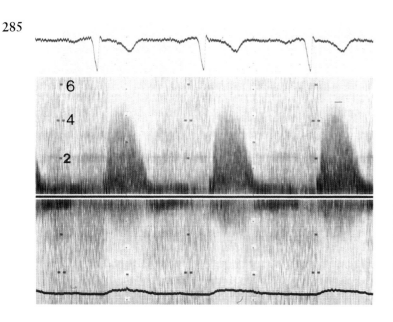

285 Continuous wave Doppler echocardiography (suprasternal view). Degeneration of homograft and xenograft valve replacements may result in valvular stenosis. In this example, there is a gradient of more than 100 mmHg across an aortic valve homograft.

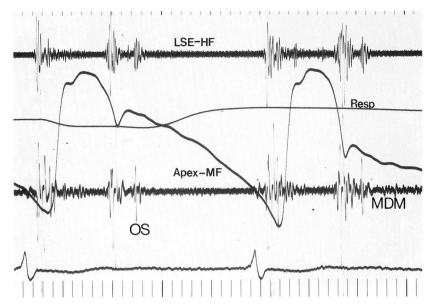

286

286 Phonocardiogram and carotid impulse in a patient with mitral stenosis following mitral valvotomy. The opening snap (os) is loud but late and there is a mid-diastolic murmur (MDM).

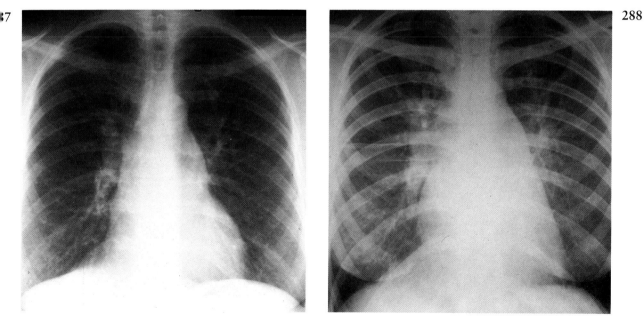

287 & 288 Chest radiographs showing a patient following mitral valvotomy (**287**). Subsequently, with the development of mitral restenosis, this patient developed left ventricular failure (**288**).

101

289

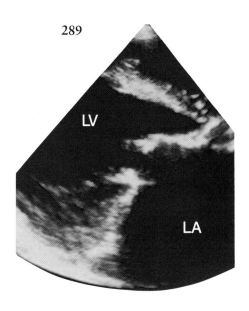

290

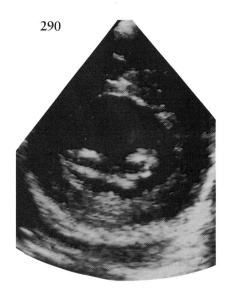

289 & 290 Cross sectional echocardiogram (parasternal long axis view **289**, short axis view **290**). Following mitral valvotomy, the mitral valve orifice is moderately large but the valve retains its thickened and immobile appearance. LA – left atrium; LV – left ventricle.

291

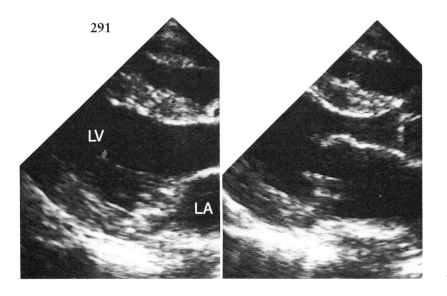

291 Cross sectional echocardiogram (parasternal long axis view; systole left, diastole right). Following mitral valve repair for floppy valve, the valve remained regurgitant and there was mitral stenosis. Left ventricular function was poor and heart failure developed. LA – left atrium; LV – left ventricle.

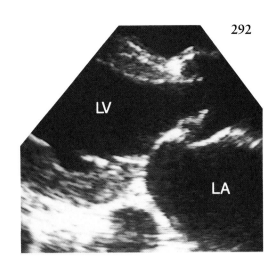

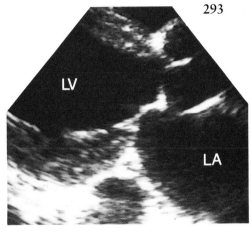

292 & 293 Cross sectional echocardiogram (parasternal long axis view; systole **292**, diastole **293**). Following mitral valve repair for severe mitral regurgitation, poor left ventricular function is a common problem. In this patient although the valve is competent, left ventricular function is sufficiently poor for heart failure to persist. LA – left atrium; LV – left ventricle.

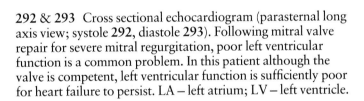

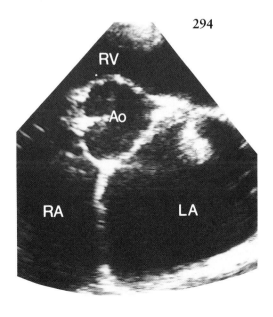

294 Cross sectional echocardiogram (parasternal short axis view). In this patient (same as in **292, 293**) heart failure is associated with accumulation of thrombus in the left atrial appendage seen in this example prolapsing into the left atrium (arrow). Ao – aorta; LA – left atrium; RA – right atrium; RV – right ventricle.

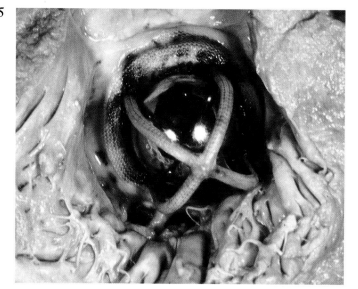

295 Macroscopic view of a Starr-Edwards mitral valve replacement viewed from the left ventricle.

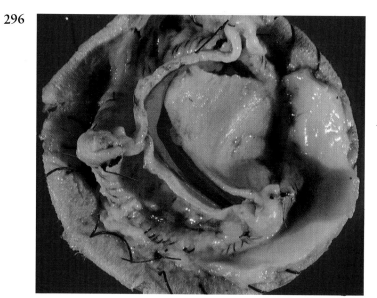

296 Excised fascia-lata valve which had become both stenosed and regurgitant.

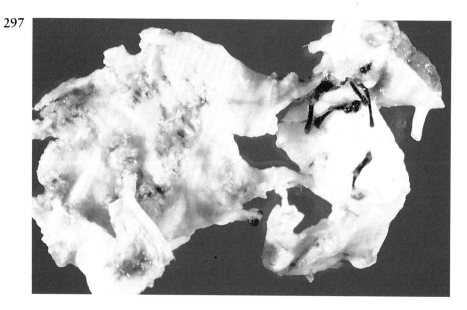

297 Excised dura mater valve which had become stenosed and regurgitant.

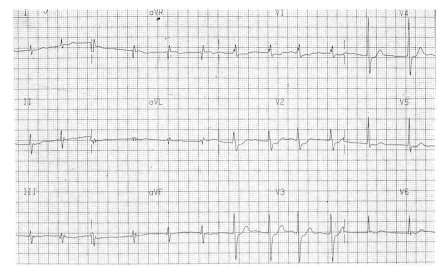

298 Electrocardiogram in a patient with a mitral valve replacement who subsequently developed left ventricular failure due to a paraprosthetic leak. There is atrial fibrillation and evidence of right ventricular hypertrophy.

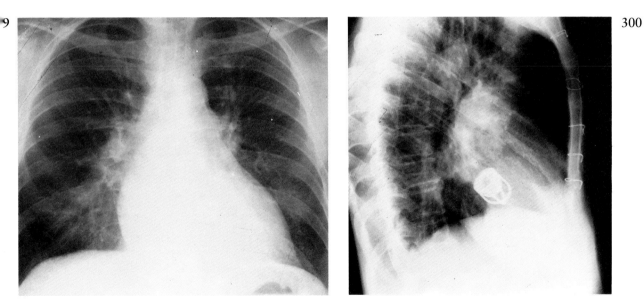

299 & 300 Chest radiograph (postero-anterior projection **299**, lateral projection **300**) showing pulmonary oedema secondary to a paraprosthetic leak following a Starr-Edwards mitral valve replacement.

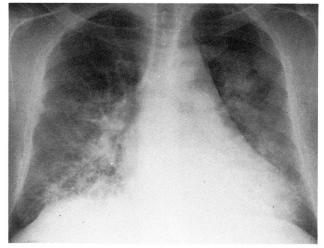

301 Chest radiograph showing pulmonary oedema secondary to mitral restenosis of a mitral valve xenograft.

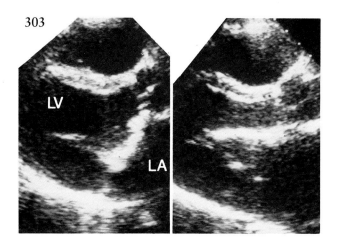

302 Chest radiograph showing a grossly enlarged heart with poor left ventricular function following mitral valve replacement with a Braunwald-Cutter valve. Although the patient was not in overt pulmonary oedema, his cardiac output was low.

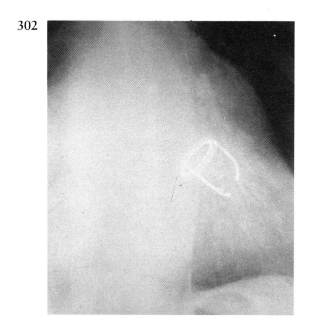

303 & 304 Cross sectional (**303**) and M-mode echocardiogram (**304**) in a patient with a failed fascia-lata mitral valve replacement (same patient as in **297**). This shows the anterior mitral valve leaflet to be thickened and move abnormally on the cross sectional echocardiogram as well as on the M-mode echocardiogram. LA – left atrium; LV – left ventricle.

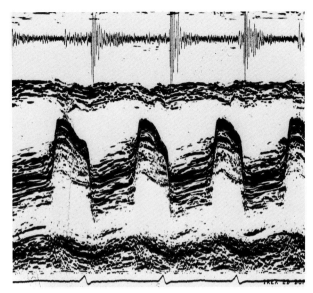

305 Doppler echocardiogram in the same patient showing restenosis of the fascia-lata mitral valve.

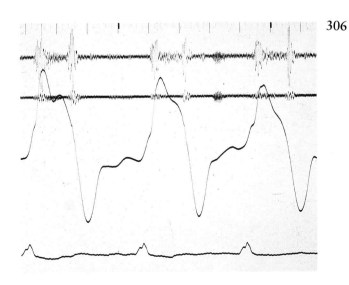

306 Phonocardiogram with apex cardiogram in a patient with restenosis of a xenograft mitral valve replacement and poor left ventricular function. The apex cardiogram has the motion suggestive of mitral stenosis (tapping apex beat) and the phonocardiogram shows systolic and mid-diastolic murmurs.

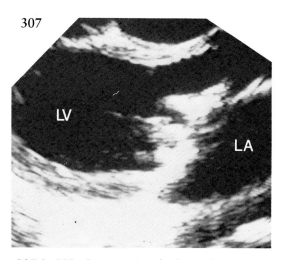

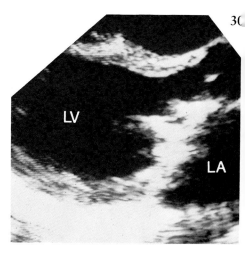

307 & 308 Cross sectional echocardiogram (parasternal long axis view; systole **307**, diastole **308**) in the same patient as (**301**) showing poor left ventricular function with restenosis following mitral valve replacement. This valve is a stented xenograft and there is thickening of the valve cusps. LA – left atrium; LV – left ventricle.

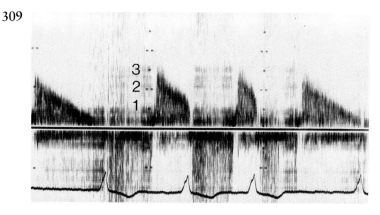

309 Continuous wave Doppler echocardiogram (apical view) showing restenosis of a mitral valve xenograft with regurgitation.

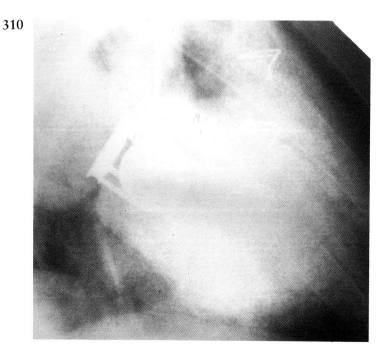

310 Left ventricular angiogram (right anterior oblique projection) showing severe mitral regurgitation around a Starr-Edwards mitral valve replacement.

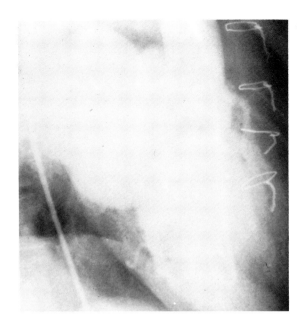

311 Left ventricular angiogram (right anterior oblique projection) showing a severely regurgitant fascia-lata mitral valve (same patient as **297, 303** and **304**).

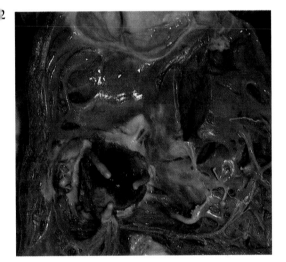

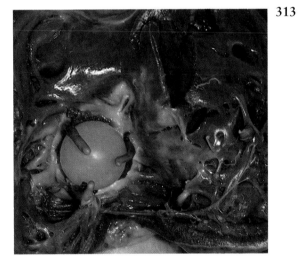

312 & 313 Macroscopic view of a Braunwald-Cutter valve in the tricuspid position. This valve in life had become thrombosed causing obstruction and leading to severe right heart failure.

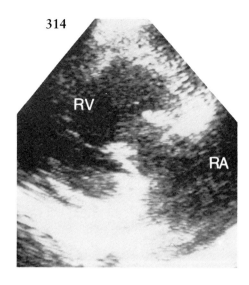

314 Cross sectional echocardiogram (right ventricular long axis view). This shows a tricuspid valve xenograft. In this example, function of the valve is normal. RA – right atrium; RV – right ventricle.

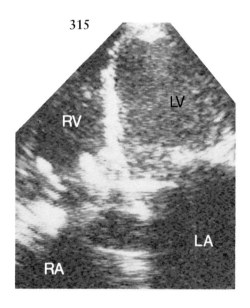

315 Cross sectional echocardiogram (apical long axis view). This shows a tricuspid valve xenograft. Although the stent of the valve can be seen well, the cusps are not visualised. LA – left atrium; LV – left ventricle; RA – right atrium; RV – right ventricle.

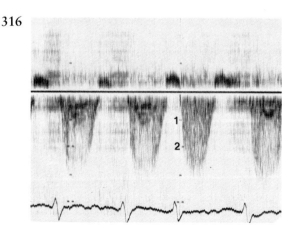

316 Continuous wave Doppler echocardiogram (apical view). Bioprosthetic tricuspid valve replacements become predominantly regurgitant and this can be easily visualised by Doppler echocardiography. In this example, the peak velocity of blood across the tricuspid orifice is 3 M/s suggesting that the right ventricular systolic pressure is normal.

IV HEART MUSCLE DISEASE

Dilated cardiomyopathy

Idiopathic dilated cardiomyopathy is defined as a dilated left ventricle, poor left ventricular function and heart failure due to primary heart muscle disease. In many cases there is no known cause but it has been suggested that previous viral myocarditis may be responsible. A similar syndrome may occur acutely during myocarditis or within weeks of the infection. Other causes include alcoholism, rheumatic fever, myxoedema, acromegaly, the storage disorders, sarcoidosis, phaeochromocytoma, renal failure, neuromuscular conditions, adriamycin toxicity and scleroderma. Rarely, dilated cardiomyopathy may occur during pregnancy.

Anaemia, particularly in association with iron deposition in the heart will lead to heart failure; the most important conditions causing this include thalassaemia and sickle cell anaemia.

All of these conditions present with a similar clinical syndrome. The electrocardiogram will show non-specific changes but these may be anterior Q waves simulating a myocardial infarction, left bundle branch block pattern or left ventricular hypertrophy. The development of atrial fibrillation is common and may exacerbate the heart failure. The chest x-ray will show an enlarged heart and evidence of pulmonary venous congestion. The echocardiogram is the non-invasive investigation of choice showing a dilated left ventricle with generalised poor contraction and possibly an associated pericardial effusion. Invasive investigations serve only to confirm poor left ventricular function and to document the absence of coronary artery disease. The prognosis in this condition is poor. As it often affects young people, cardiac transplantation improves both the morbidity and the mortality. Heart muscle disease due to known causes will, of course, have physical signs which will reflect the underlying condition.

318

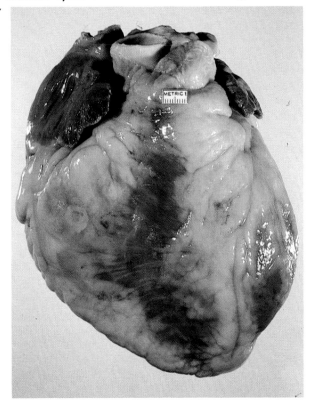 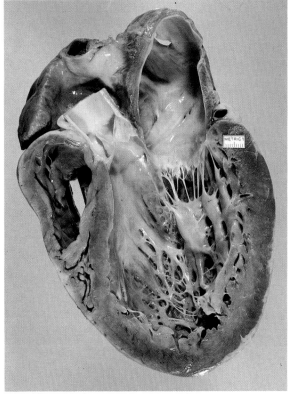

317 & 318 Macroscopic view of the heart in dilated cardiomyopathy (**317**). The heart is enlarged and the long axis view (**318**) shows a grossly dilated right and left ventricular cavity.

319

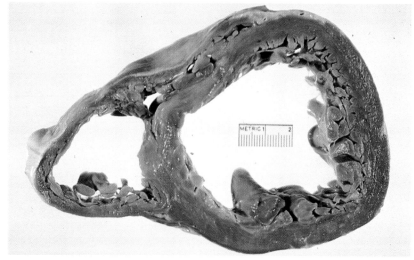

319 Macroscopic section (transverse view) through the ventricles in idiopathic dilated cardiomyopathy. Both ventricular cavities are grossly dilated but the ventricular walls are not hypertrophied.

320

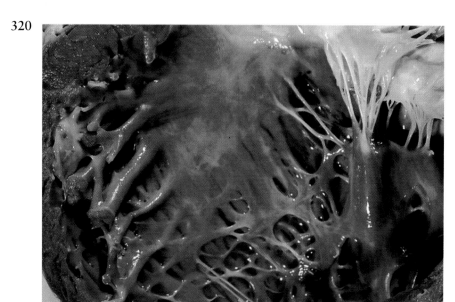

320 Macroscopic view of a dilated left ventricular cavity in idiopathic dilated cardiomyopathy. The white areas of fibrosis overlying the endocardium are related to local thrombosis secondary to blood stasis and are commonly seen.

321

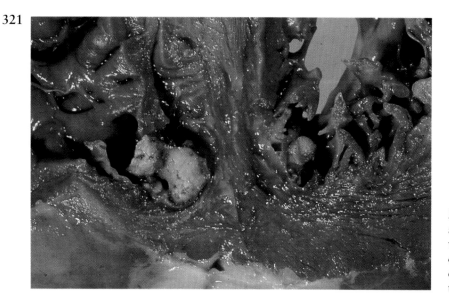

321 Macroscopic view of the apices of the left and right ventricles in idiopathic dilated cardiomyopathy showing calcified thrombi within the trabeculae of each ventricle.

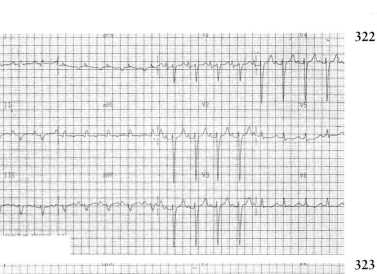

322

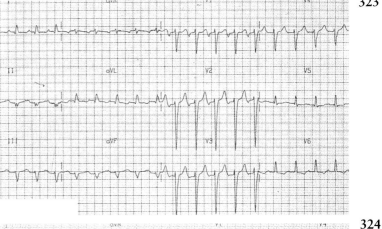

323

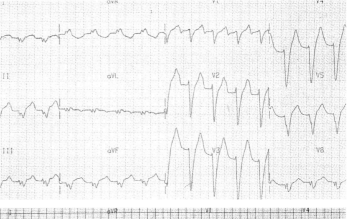

324

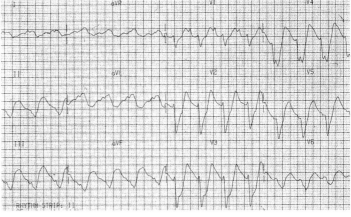

325

322-325 Series of electrocardiograms in idiopathic dilated cardiomyopathy showing initially (322) left atrial enlargement, left ventricular hypertrophy with repolarisation changes; there is subsequently progressive prolongation of the QRS complex (323-325). The final electrocardiogram preceded death by only 24 hours.

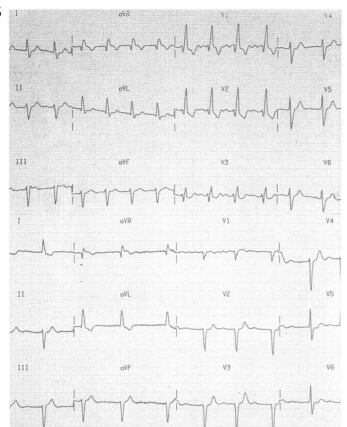

326 Electrocardiograms in idiopathic dilated cardiomyopathy showing the typical myocardial infarct pattern of anterior Q waves. There is also a right bundle branch block pattern (above). Changes in the electrocardiogram are common in idiopathic dilated cardiomyopathy and shown here (below) is the subsequent development of left bundle branch block indicating further myocardial damage.

327

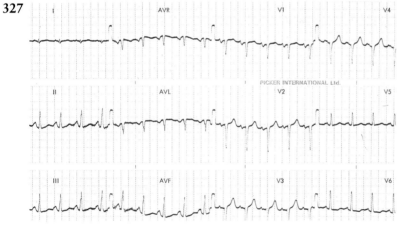

328

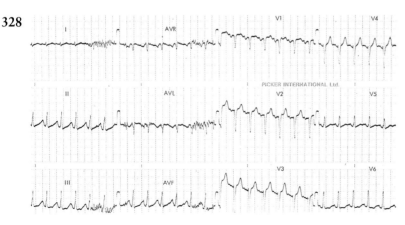

327 & 328 Exercise electrocardiogram in dilated cardiomyopathy showing typical Q wave pattern at rest (**327**) with no changes in the ST segments on effort though a rapid rise in heart rate occurred at a low work load (**328**).

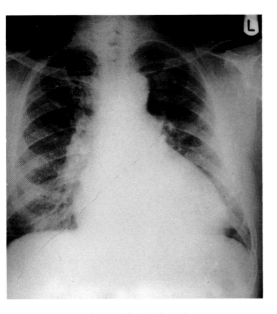

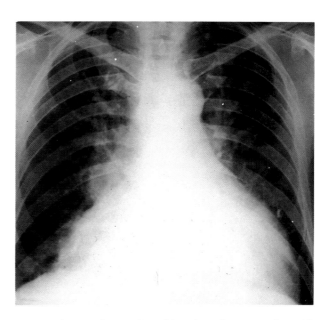

329 Chest radiograph in dilated cardiomyopathy showing a grossly enlarged heart with evidence of pulmonary venous congestion.

330 Chest radiograph in dilated cardiomyopathy with pulmonary oedema. The heart is grossly enlarged.

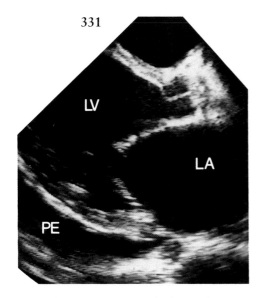

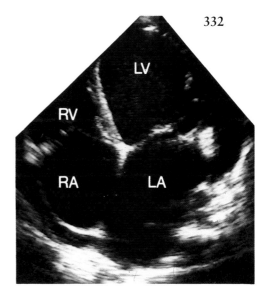

331 & 332 Cross sectional echocardiogram (parasternal long axis view **331**, apical long axis view **332**). The left ventricle is dilated and in real time can be seen to be poorly contracting. There is in addition a posterior pericardial effusion (PE). The myocardium is thin. In the long axis apical view it can be seen that the left ventricle (LV) is rounded in appearance. LA – left atrium; RA – right atrium; RV – right ventricle.

333

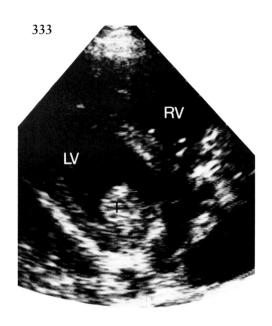

334

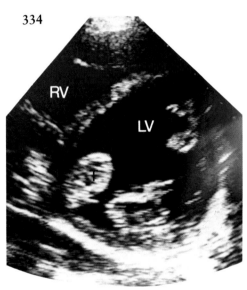

333 & 334 Cross sectional echocardiogram (parasternal long axis view **333**, short axis view **334**). The development of left ventricular thrombus is common in dilated cardiomyopathy and is related to the poor cardiac output. In this patient, prior to cardiac transplantation, multiple pedunculated poorly moving thrombi (T) can be seen lying within the left ventricular cavity around the mitral valve ring. LV – left ventricle; RV – right ventricle.

335

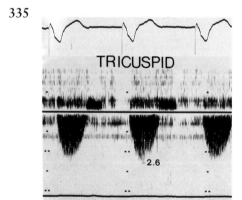 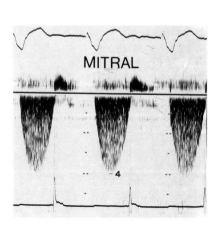

335 Continuous wave Doppler echocardiogram. From the apex, both tricuspid and mitral regurgitation can be demonstrated in patients with dilated cardiomyopathy. Such regurgitation is due to ventricular dilatation.

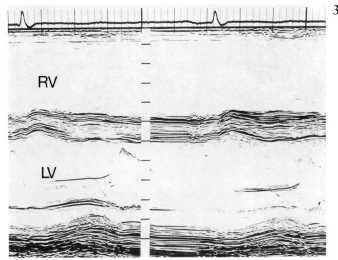
336

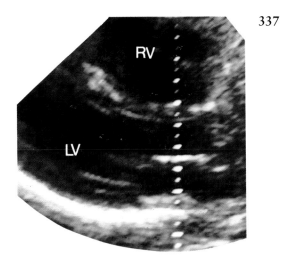
337

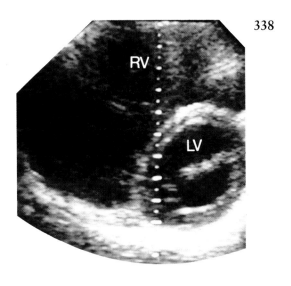
338

336-338 M-mode echocardiogram and cross sectional echocardiogram (336), (parasternal long axis view 337, short axis view 338). In right ventricular cardiomyopathy, the right ventricle (RV) is dilated as can be seen on the M-mode and both cross sectional echocardiograms with poor contraction. The left ventricle (LV) is not dilated, but has some impairment of its contraction pattern.

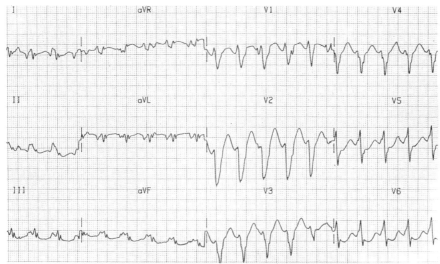

339 Electrocardiogram. The development of ventricular tachycardia is common in right ventricular cardiomyopathy and may be its presenting symptom.

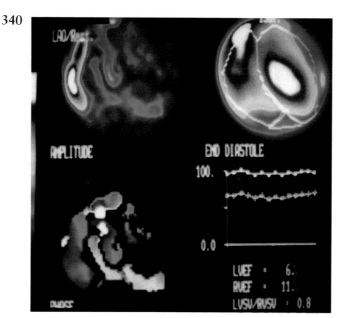

340 Gated blood pool scan in dilated cardiomyopathy showing a dilated end-diastolic image of the left ventricle (top right), global hypokinesis on the amplitude image (top left) and a discrete area of dyskinesia at the left ventricular apex on the phase image (bottom left). The left and right ventricular volume time curve show a left ventricular ejection fraction of 6% and right ventricular ejection fraction of 11% (bottom right).

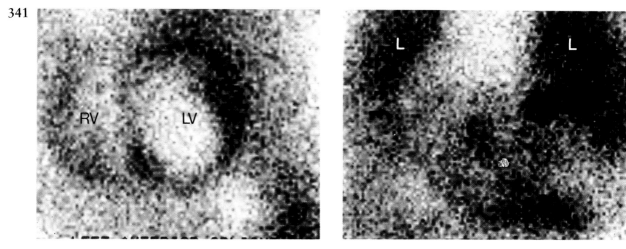

341 & 342 Thallium scintigrams (anteroposterior **341**, left anterior oblique **342**) showing intense uptake of thallium in both lung fields (L) due to pulmonary oedema (**341**). Both ventricles are dilated and there is patchy distribution of thallium uptake (**342**). LV – left ventricle; RV – right ventricle.

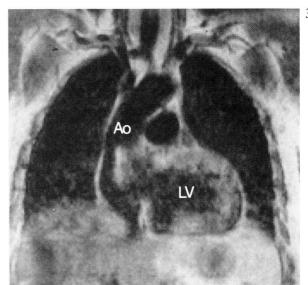

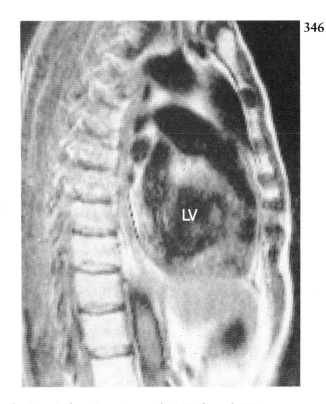

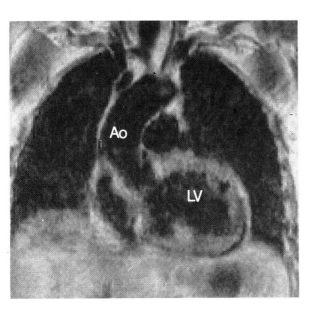

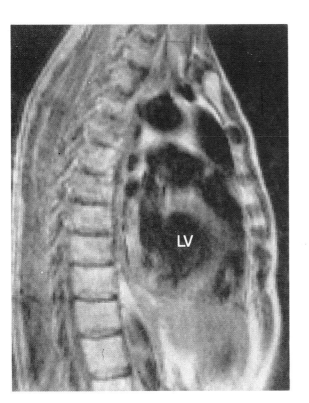

343-346 Magnetic resonance scans in dilated cardiomyopathy (saggital sections in systole **343**, diastole **344**; coronal sections in systole **345**, and diastole **346**) showing a grossly hypertrophied left ventricle (LV) which contracts poorly. Ao – aorta.

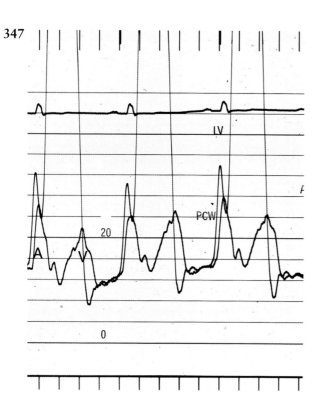

347 Haemodynamic tracing showing simultaneous wedge and left ventricular end-diastolic pressure. There is no gradient across the mitral valve and the wedge pressure, reflecting left atrial pressure, is elevated showing prominent A and V waves.

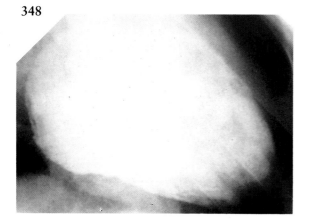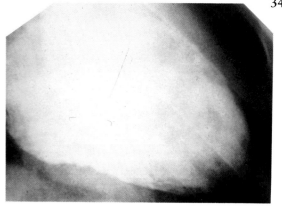

348 & 349 Left ventricular angiograms in dilated cardiomyopathy (systole **348**, diastole **349**) showing poor left ventricular function. In contrast to ischaemic heart disease, there are no regional abnormalities.

350

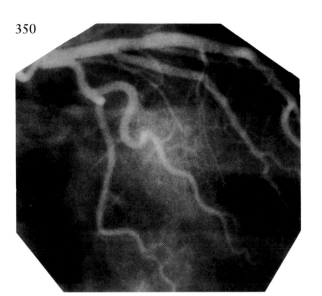

351

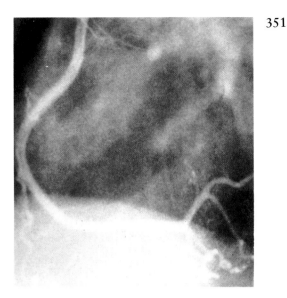

350 & 351 Coronary arteriography is essential to differentiate dilated cardiomyopathy from generalised damage of the left ventricle due to ischaemic heart disease. In dilated cardiomyopathy both the left (**350**) and the right (**351**) coronary arteries are normal.

352

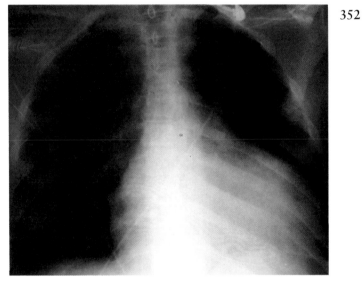

353

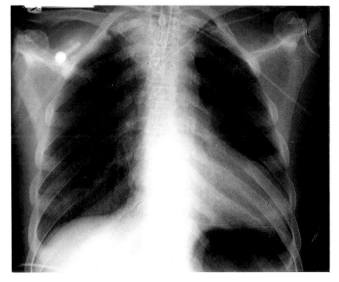

352 & 353 Chest radiographs from a patient with dilated cardiomyopathy before (**352**) and after (**353**) orthotopic cardiac transplantation. Orthotopic transplantation is where the patient's heart is replaced by the donor heart.

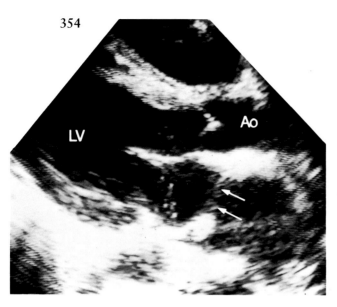

354 Cross sectional echocardiogram (parasternal long axis view) showing the anastomosis (arrows) of the donor and recipient left atrium following orthotopic transplantation. Ao – aorta; LV – left ventricle.

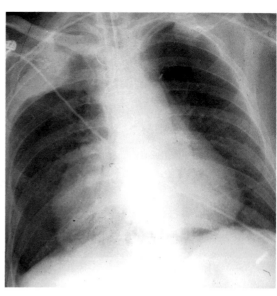

355 Chest radiograph in dilated cardiomyopathy after heterotopic cardiac transplantation in which, in addition to the patient's own heart, a further heart was inserted as a left ventricular assist.

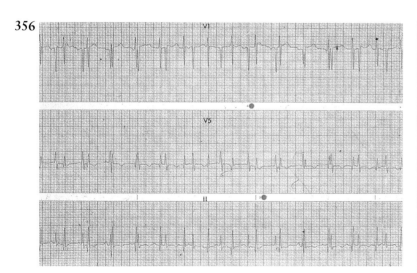

356 Electrocardiogram after heterotopic cardiac transplantation showing the electrocardiographic pattern of the two hearts beating.

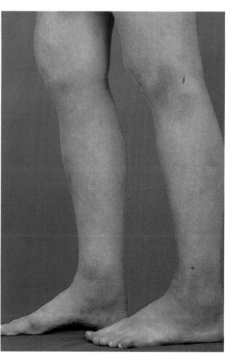

357 Classically, rheumatic fever presents with swollen tender joints as shown here.

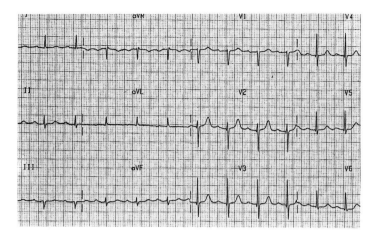

358 Electrocardiogram in rheumatic fever will often show first degree atrioventricular block.

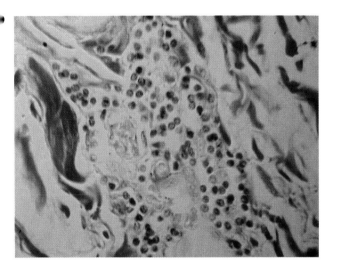

359 Histology of amputated left atrial appendage with an Aschoff node in rheumatic fever.

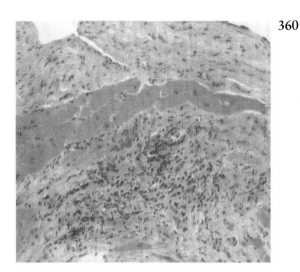

360 Left ventricular biopsy specimen showing acute viral myocarditis. There is fibrosis of myocardium (top) with a lymphocytic infiltrate (below).

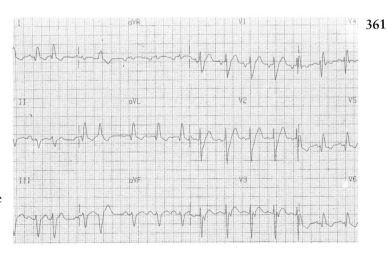

361 The electrocardiographic changes in myocarditis are non-specific. In this example there is left atrial enlargement with bundle branch block and widespread ST segment change.

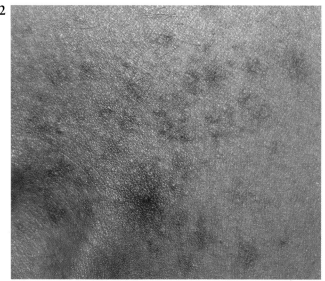

362 Spider naevi are common in alcoholics as shown here on the chest of a patient with alcoholic heart disease who was in heart failure.

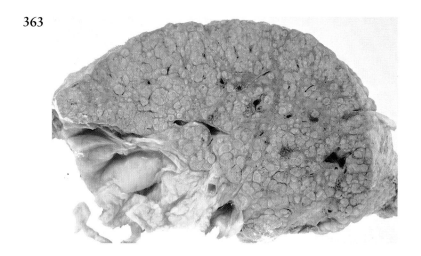

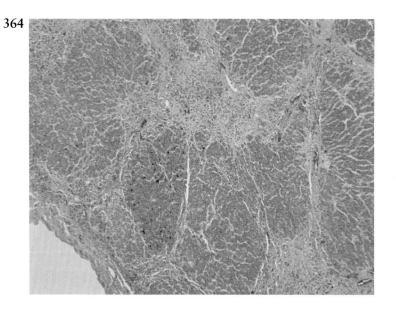

363 & 364 Pathological specimens showing macro-nodulous cirrhosis (363) and micro-nodular cirrhosis (364) in patients with alcoholic heart disease who had associated alcoholic cirrhosis of the liver. Alcoholic heart disease often occurs in association with liver disease, but the two do not necessarily go together and liver function can be normal in patients with advanced heart disease.

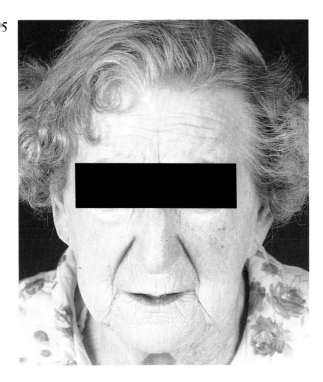

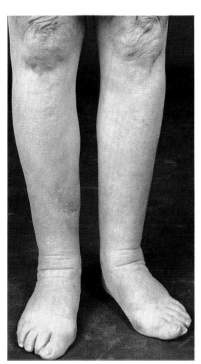

365 & 366 Clinical photographs in myxoedema in a patient with associated heart disease showing the typical myxoedema facies (**365**) and pretibial myxoedema (**366**).

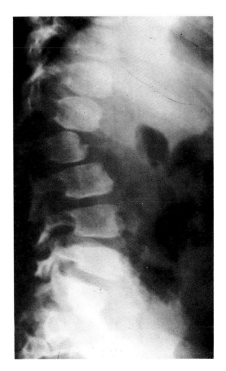

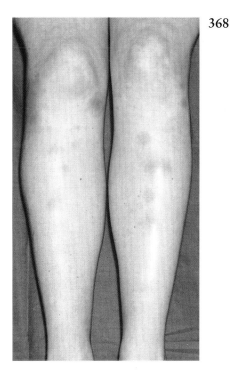

367 Connective tissue diseases such as Hurler's syndrome develop cardiac infiltration leading to heart failure. This example of Hurler's syndrome shows the typical spinal abnormality of spinal collapse with gibbus formation.

368 Clinical photograph showing erythema nodosum in a patient with sarcoid heart disease and heart failure.

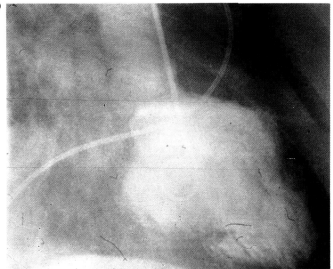
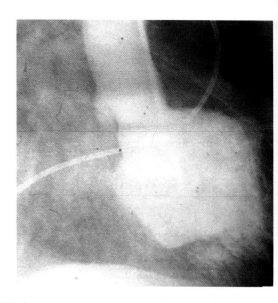

369 & 370 Left ventricular angiogram (systole **369**, diastole **370**) showing the characteristic features of cardiac sarcoid with basal hypokinesis and preserved apical function.

371

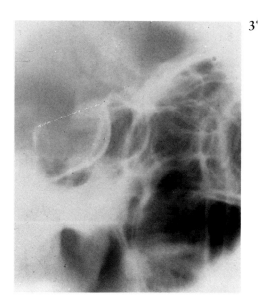

3

371 Hand radiograph in sarcoid showing bony erosion. Erythema nodosum as in **368** occurs in early sarcoidosis and is rarely associated with heart disease; in contrast, bony erosion is a late phenomena and is more commonly associated with heart disease.

372 Coned lateral skull radiograph in a patient with acromegaly with enlargement of the pituitary fossa and a double floor.

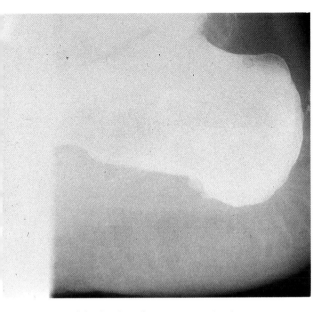

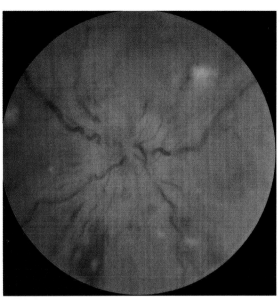

373 X-ray of the heel pad in acromegaly showing thickening of the soft tissues.

374 Retinal fundus showing papilloedema in phaeochromocytoma. Heart failure may occur in phaeochromocytoma not only because of hypertension but also because of catecholamine induced myocarditis.

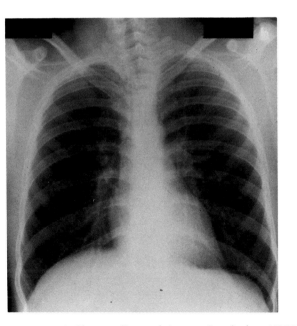

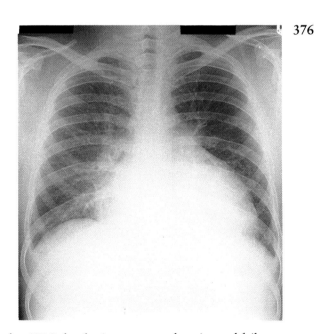

375 & 376 Chest radiograph in a patient before (**375**) and after (**376**) developing acute on chronic renal failure. The renal failure caused impairment of left ventricular function, the development of a pericardial effusion and heart failure which is evident on the chest radiograph. Such changes are largely reversible using renal dialysis or renal transplantation.

377

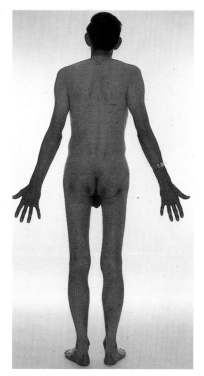 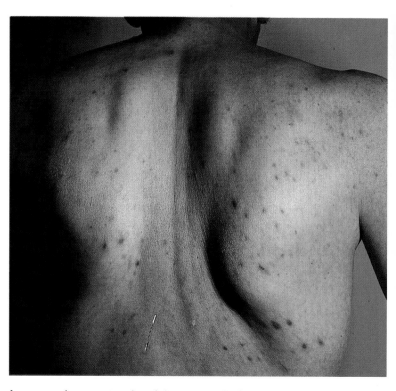

377 & 378 Neuromuscular disorders are known to be associated with heart muscle disease. These clinical photographs show muscle wasting associated with weakness in a patient with skeletal myopathy who also had heart failure with heart muscle disease. In this patient, there was a dilated left ventricle and the electrocardiogram showed left bundle branch block.

379

379 Cross sectional echocardiogram (parasternal long axis view; systole left, diastole right). In Friedreich's ataxia, septal hypertrophy is common and the appearances of hypertrophic cardiomyopathy may be seen. In this example, there is septal hypertrophy and in addition there is dilatation of the left ventricle (LV) with poor contraction. PW – posterior wall; VS – ventricular septum.

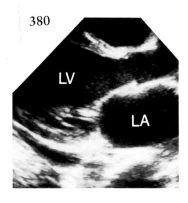

380 Cross sectional echocardiogram (parasternal long axis view) in adriamycin cardiomyopathy. There is characteristically thinning of the myocardium associated with poor left ventricular function. LA – left atrium; LV – left ventricle.

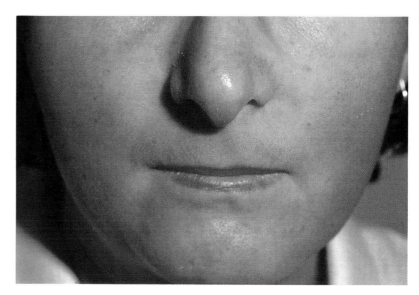

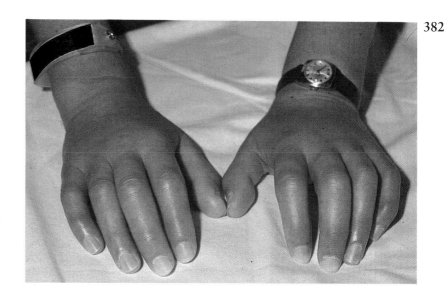

381 & 382 Clinical photographs in scleroderma showing a taut and thickened skin around the mouth (**381**) and involving the fingers of the hands (**382**). There is also oedema of the hands.

383 Cross sectional echocardiogram (parasternal long axis view). The echocardiogram in scleroderma frequently shows pericardial thickening often with a small pericardial effusion (E), left ventricular hypertrophy is usually due to coexistent hypertension and there may be impairment of left ventricular diastolic function. Only very occasionally is there left ventricular dilatation. Ao – aorta; LA – left atrium; LV – left ventricle.

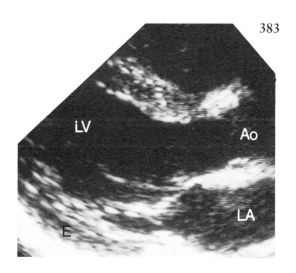

384

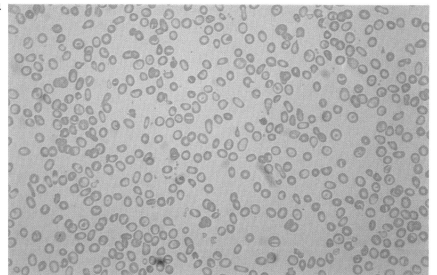

384 Blood film in thalassaemia showing hypochromic microcytic red cells which are flattened; in addition there are target cells.

385

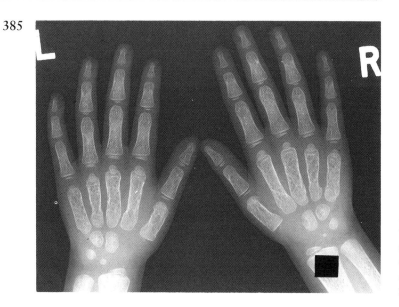

385 Hand x-ray in thalassaemia showing enlargement of the marrow cavity and thinning of cortical bone with abnormal trabeculations.

386

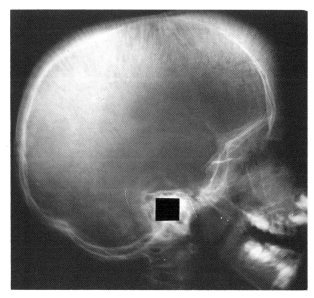

386 Lateral skull radiograph showing 'hair-on-end' appearance in thalassaemia due to enlargement of the marrow cavity.

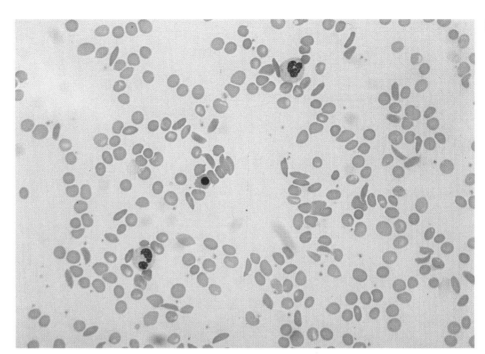

387 Blood film in sickle cell anaemia showing nucleated red cells. The sickle cells can also be seen.

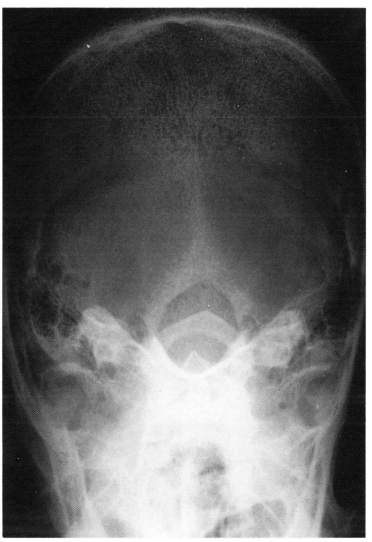

388 Skull radiograph in sickle cell anaemia showing widening of the marrow cavity and elevation of the periosteum.

Hypertrophic Cardiomyopathy

Hypertrophic cardiomyopathy is a rare cause of heart failure. The diagnosis of hypertrophic cardiomyopathy rests on the presence of asymmetrical or concentric hypertrophy of the left ventricle without an underlying cause. Clinically such patients usually present with angina pectoris, palpitations or syncope and only rarely with symptoms due to heart failure. Heart failure is predominantly due to an abnormality of diastolic function of the left ventricle with abnormal relaxation and slow filling causing a rise in left atrial pressure. It may be exacerbated by the associated presence of mitral regurgitation or the development of cardiac arrhythmias. Patients with hypertrophic cardiomyopathy in heart failure usually do not have a gradient within the left ventricular cavity. However, following myotomy, myectomy or mitral valve replacement, heart failure is an important complication.

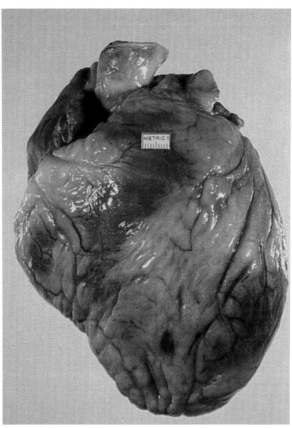
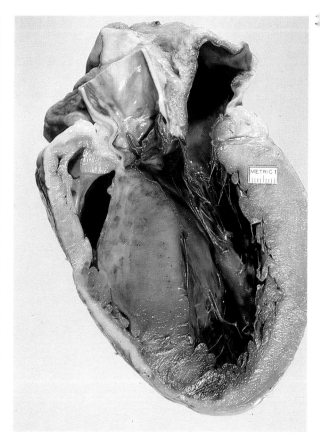

389 & 390 External appearance of the heart in hypertrophic cardiomyopathy. There is marked increase in weight due to left ventricular hypertrophy (**389**). In the long axis echo view (**390**) there is gross left ventricular hypertrophy more marked in the septum than in the free wall.

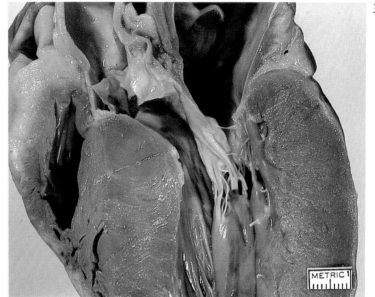

391 Long axis section in hypertrophic cardiomyopathy. Both the septum and left ventricular free wall are markedly thickened and the outflow tract is narrow. An area of white thickened endocardium overlies the bulging septum due to contact with the anterior leaflet of the mitral valve ('contact lesion').

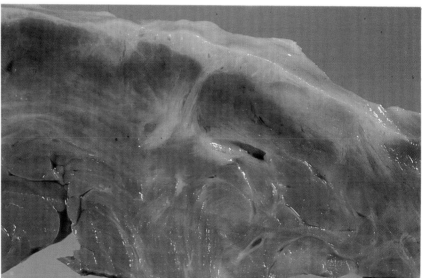

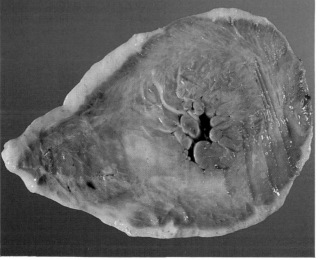

392 & 393 Left ventricular wall in hypertrophic cardiomyopathy (**392**). There is a transmural scar with normal epicardial coronary arteries. Cross sections through the left and right ventricles (**393**) close to the apex show extensive transmural fibrosis.

394

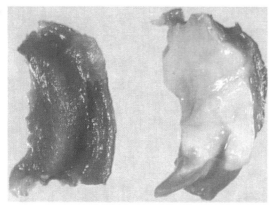

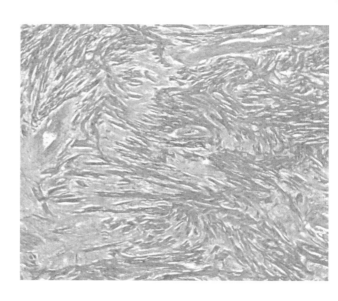

394 Excised left ventricular septal muscle from a patient with hypertrophic cardiomyopathy who underwent a myotomy and myectomy. The thickened white endocardium occurs at the point of contact between the septum and mitral valve during systole.

396

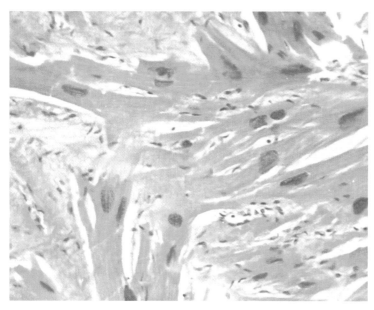

395 & 396 Histological section of the left ventricular septum in hypertrophic cardiomyopathy (**395**). There is marked fibre disarray and areas of fibrosis between the fibres (H and E × 20). High power view of a histological section of left ventricular septum showing hypertrophied, malaligned fibres with large nuclei (**396**) (H and E × 100).

397

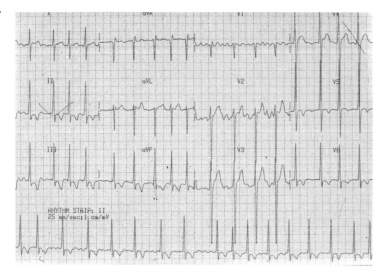

397 Electrocardiogram in hypertrophic cardiomyopathy in heart failure showing severe left ventricular hypertrophy; the rhythm is atrial fibrillation. Atrial fibrillation frequently precipitates heart failure in such patients.

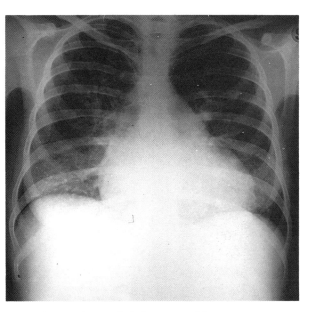

398 Chest radiograph in hypertrophic cardiomyopathy showing a grossly enlarged left ventricle and pulmonary venous congestion.

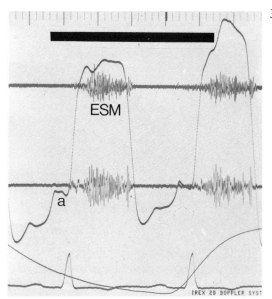

399 Phonocardiogram and apex cardiogram showing a loud systolic ejection murmur and a sustained apex cardiogram with accentuated atrial contraction (a).

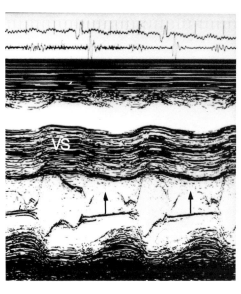

400 M-mode echocardiogram showing a grossly thickened interventricular septum (VS) of 3 cm (normal up to 1.2 cm). There is, in addition, systolic anterior motion of the mitral valve (arrow). The left ventricle is small but contracts normally.

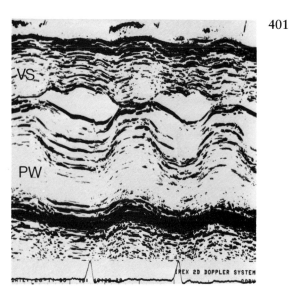

401

401 M-mode echocardiogram in a patient with hypertrophic cardiomyopathy and heart failure (same patient as **397**). In this example there is atrial fibrillation and the left ventricle is grossly hypertrophied with a tiny cavity which eliminates at end-systole. PW – posterior wall; VS – ventricular septum.

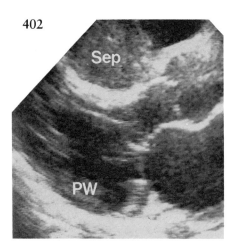

402 Cross sectional echocardiogram (parasternal long axis view) showing a grossly thickened septum (Sep) which is also considerably thicker than the posterior wall (PW). In this example, the left ventricular cavity is small and the left atrium enlarged.

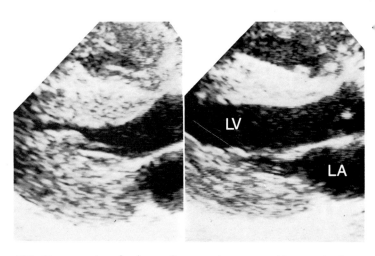

403 Cross sectional echocardiogram (parasternal long axis view; systole left, diastole right). Heart failure may ensue in hypertrophic cardiomyopathy when the left ventricle (LV) is small and hypercontractile as in this example. LA – left atrium.

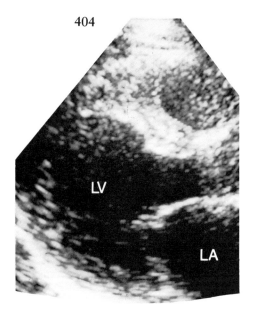

404 Cross sectional echocardiogram (parasternal long axis view). Rarely, heart failure may ensue in hypertrophic cardiomyopathy when dilatation of the left ventricle occurs. This may occur due to myocardial infarction or extension of the heart muscle disease. In this example, although the septum remains thickened, there is dilatation and poor contraction of the left ventricle (LV). LA – left atrium.

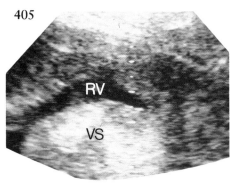

405 Cross sectional echocardiogram (parasternal short axis view, magnified). Severe right ventricular hypertrophy may readily be seen by cross sectional echocardiography and may be the cause of right heart failure. RV – right ventricle; VS – ventricular septum.

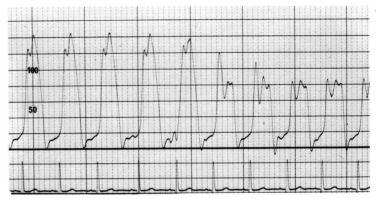

406 Haemodynamic trace in hypertrophic cardiomyopathy showing a sub-aortic gradient within the left ventricle. Usually, by the time the patient presents with heart failure, this gradient is no longer evident.

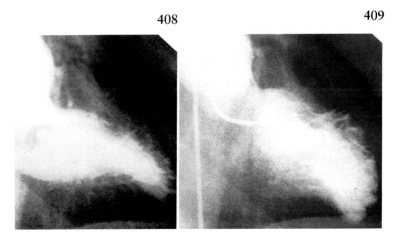

407 Magnetic resonance scan (systole above, diastole below) in hypertrophic cardiomyopathy showing a grossly thickened left ventricle (LV) involving the septum. The hypertrophied papillary muscles within the left ventricle can be seen. RV – right ventricle.

408 & 409 Left ventricular angiogram (systole **408**, diastole **409**) in hypertrophic cardiomyopathy showing a hypertrophied left ventricle with good contraction. In patients with hypertrophic cardiomyopathy who develop heart failure, systolic function may well remain normal or even hyperdynamic. The cause of the heart failure is due to diastolic abnormalities of relaxation and filling.

410

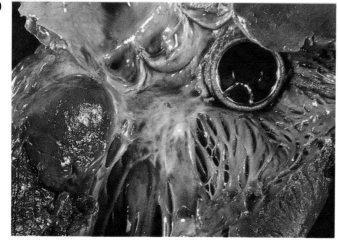

410 Pathological specimen showing a Björk-Shiley mitral valve replacement in hypertrophic cardiomyopathy.

411

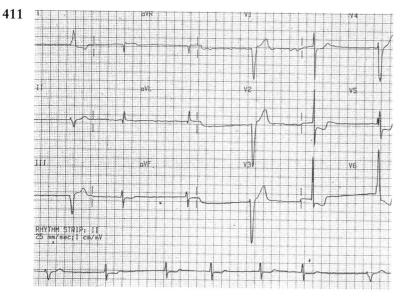

411 Following myotomy, the electrocardiogram frequently shows a left bundle branch block pattern. In addition, in this patient with heart failure, there is bradycardia and atrial fibrillation.

412

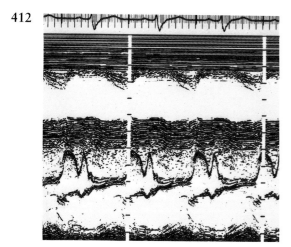

413

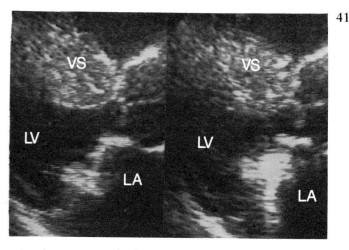

412 M-mode echocardiogram. Following myotomy and myectomy the left ventricular outflow tract gradient is lost but the left ventricular cavity may be enlarged and the function impaired.

413 Cross sectional echocardiogram (parasternal long axis view; systole right, diastole left). There is septal hypertrophy with good left ventricular function. Although there is a normally functioning Starr-Edwards mitral valve, the patient remained in heart failure because of abnormalities of diastolic function. LA – left atrium; LV – left ventricle; VS – ventricular septum.

Restrictive Cardiomyopathy

Restrictive cardiomyopathy is characterised by a restriction of diastolic filling due to endocardial and/or myocardial lesions. Amyloid infiltration is probably the most important cause in the UK, but endomyocardial fibrosis with or without eosinophilia is the most common world wide. Restrictive cardiomyopathy can also occur without a specific aetiology.

The presenting symptoms are usually dyspnoea with ankle or abdominal swelling. Ascites may be more marked than peripheral oedema. The physical signs include evidence of restrictive filling of the right ventricle with an elevated jugular venous pressure which may be further elevated by deep inspiration, peripheral oedema and ascites with an enlarged liver. The cardiac output may be low and there is usually a gallop rhythm on auscultation.

The most important non-invasive investigation is the echocardiogram but haemodynamics may be necessary to confirm the presence of restriction.

414

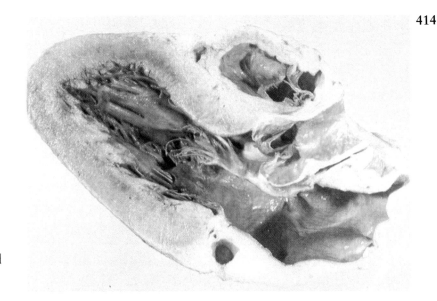

414 Long axis of the heart in amyloidosis. The heart is enlarged and the myocardium has a rubbery consistency.

415

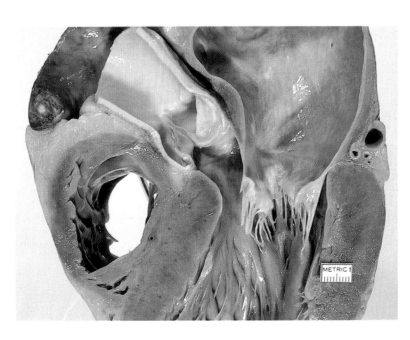

415 & 416 Long axis section of the heart in amyloidosis (**415**). Both the left atrium and the left ventricle are dilated. Macroscopic view (**416**) of the left atrium showing focal amyloid deposits on the mural endocardium which are typically tan coloured and have a waxy appearance.

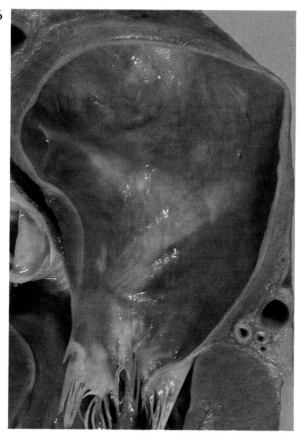

416

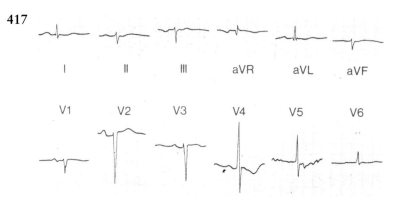

417

| I | II | III | aVR | aVL | aVF |

| V1 | V2 | V3 | V4 | V5 | V6 |

417 Electrocardiogram in amyloid heart disease. This has a characteristic appearance with small QRS voltages often with conduction abnormalities or atrial fibrillation.

418

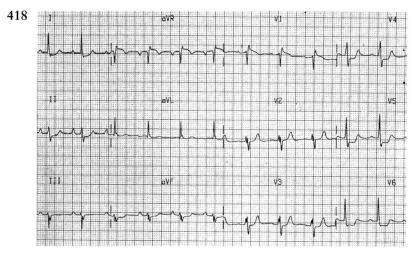

418 Electrocardiogram in eosinophilic heart disease is non-specific. In this example there is incomplete right bundle branch block with left axis deviation and widespread ST-T wave changes.

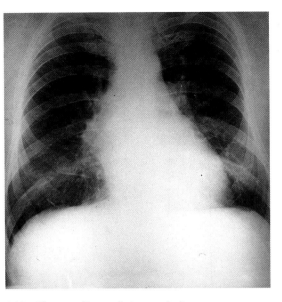

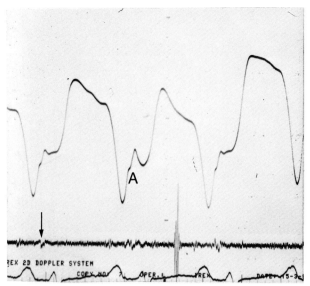

419 Chest radiograph in restrictive cardiomyopathy showing pulmonary venous congestion but the heart size is not enlarged.

420 Apex cardiogram in amyloid heart disease showing a tall A wave simultaneous with the fourth heart sound (arrow). The apex cardiogram has a 'dip and plateau' appearance similar to the ventricular pressure trace.

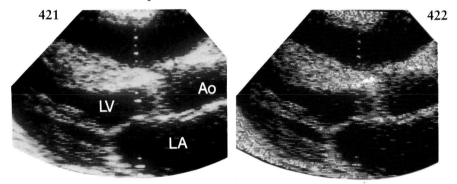

421 & 422 Cross sectional echocardiogram (parasternal long axis view) in amyloidosis. There is marked concentric left ventricular hypertrophy and a small posterior pericardial effusion (**421**). Colour encoding shows that the myocardium reflects echoes with normal intensity (**422**). This is in marked contrast to most forms of left ventricular hypertrophy where the echo intensity is increased.

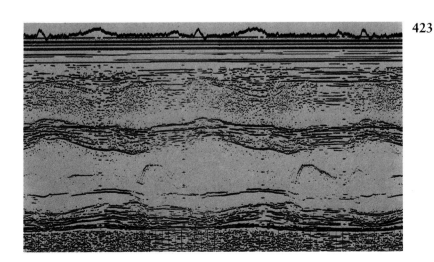

423 M-mode echocardiogram in a patient with eosinophilic heart disease. In this patient, the left ventricular cavity is not dilated, but there is poor contraction and thinning of the left ventricular posterior wall.

424

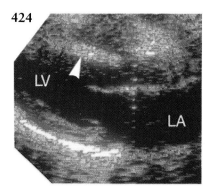

424 Colour encoded cross sectional echocardiogram (parasternal long axis view) showing bright echoes arising from the myocardium particularly from the septum (arrow) in a patient with eosinophilic heart disease. LA – left atrium; LV – left ventricle.

425

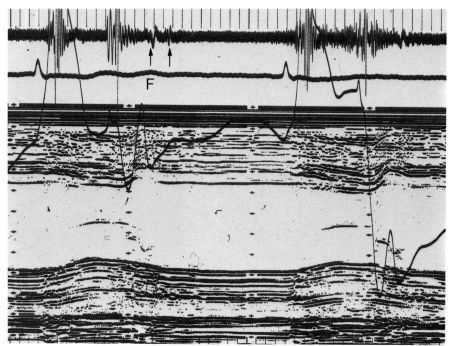

425 M-mode echocardiogram in idiopathic restrictive cardiomyopathy. In this patient there is gross posterior wall thickening without dilatation of the left ventricle. The apex cardiogram shows a marked filling wave (F) which is not simultaneous with the right and left ventricular third sounds seen on the phonocardiogram (arrows). Note that the left ventricular contraction and filling is markedly reduced.

426

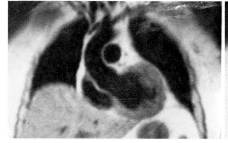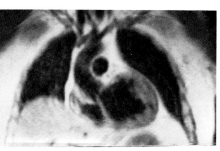

426 Magnetic resonance scan (diastole right, systole left) in amyloid heart disease showing thickening of the myocardium with preservation of left ventricular contraction.

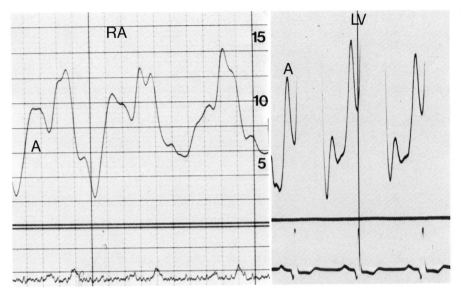

427 Haemodynamic tracing in amyloid heart disease showing the typical 'dip and plateau' appearance (right panel). The right atrial pressure will be elevated with a prominent A wave (left panel). LV – left ventricle; RA – right atrium.

428 Contrast enhanced computerised tomogram showing intracardiac thrombus (**T**) in the right ventricle and thickened pericardium (arrows) in endomyocardial disease.

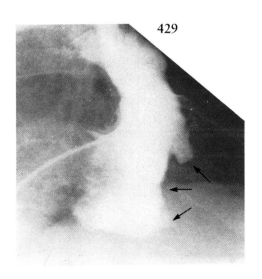

429

429 Right ventricular angiogram in eosinophilic heart disease showing obliteration of the apex with fibrous tissue (arrows).

V HYPERTENSION

Hypertension is an important cause of heart failure particularly when associated with coronary disease. However, the control of blood pressure has made heart failure a much less common complication than in the past. Hypertensive heart failure usually presents with a dilated, hypertrophied left ventricle, but occasionally the heart size may be normal and there is severe concentric hypertrophy. In these latter circumstances, the mechanism of heart failure is similar to that seen in hypertrophic cardiomyopathy.

430

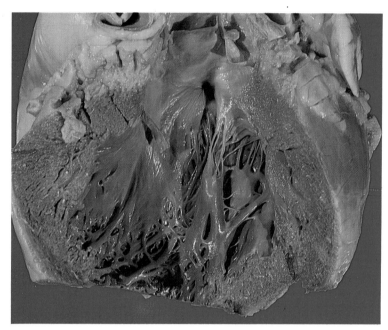

430 Dilated and hypertrophied left ventricle in hypertension with heart failure.

431

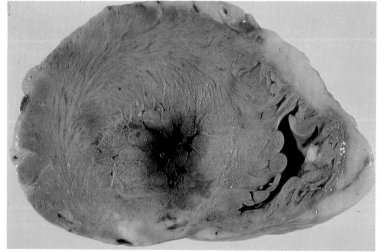

431 Macroscopic section through the left ventricle in hypertensive heart failure. There is gross left ventricular hypertrophy.

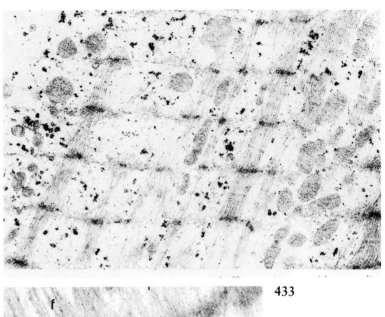

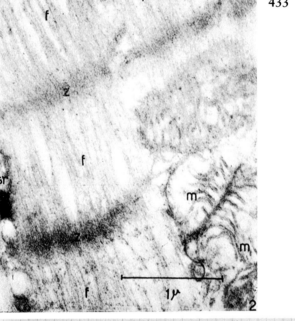

433

432 & 433 Electron micrographs of the myocardium in hypertensive heart failure. The fibres are in disarray. There is ventricular hypertrophy as shown by the increased number of mitochondria (**432**). In heart failure the mitochondria are shown to be swollen and there are also degenerative changes (**433**). SR – sarcoplasmareticulum; F – myofibril; Z – z bands; M – mitochondria.

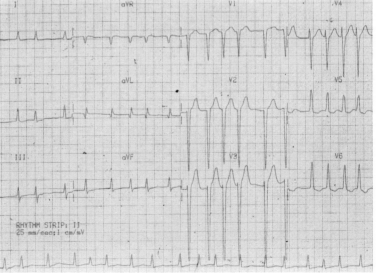

434

434 Electrocardiogram in hypertensive heart failure showing gross left ventricular hypertrophy and atrial fibrillation.

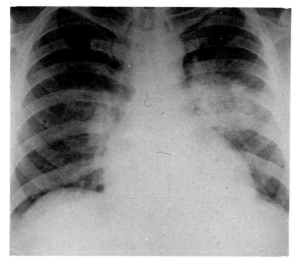

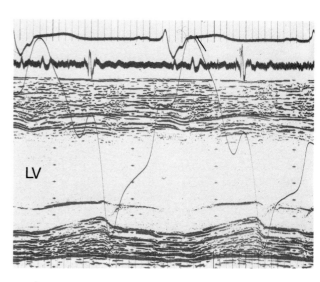

435 Chest radiograph showing a normal sized heart with severe pulmonary oedema in a patient with hypertensive heart failure.

436 M-mode echocardiogram with apex cardiogram. There is dilatation of the left ventricle (LV) with poor left ventricular contraction. There is a moderate degree of left ventricular hypertrophy.

437

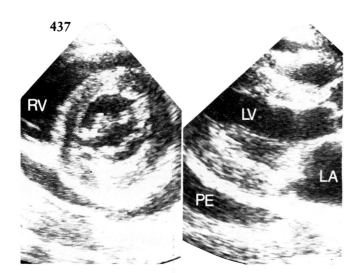

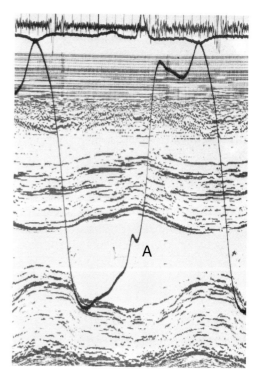

437 Cross sectional echocardiogram (parasternal short axis view left, long axis view right). Hypertrophied left ventricle (LV) with posterior pericardial effusion (PE) in a patient with hypertensive heart failure. LA – left atrium; RV – right ventricle.

438 M-mode echocardiogram in hypertension. There is concentric hypertrophy of a severe degree with a small hypercontractile left ventricular cavity. Note that there is a tall A wave in the apex cardiogram in this patient who presented with heart failure.

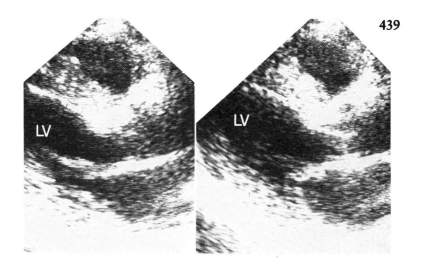

439 Cross sectional echocardiogram (parasternal long axis view; systole left, diastole right) in the same patient as **438** showing a severe degree of left ventricular hypertrophy with a small left ventricular cavity. LV – left ventricle.

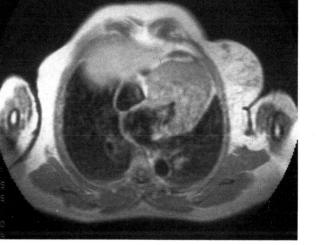

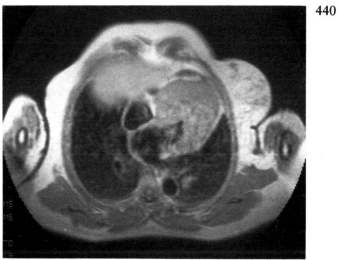

440 & 441 Magnetic resonance images (transverse sections) in systole (**440**) and diastole (**441**) in a patient with left ventricular hypertrophy due to hypertension. LA – left atrium; LV – left ventricle.

442

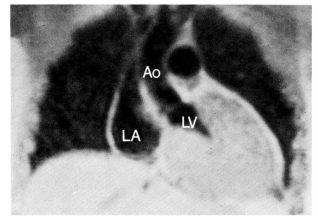

443

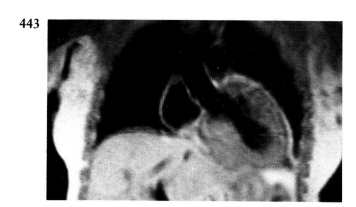

442 & 443 Magnetic resonance images (coronal sections) showing gross left ventricular hypertrophy (systole **442**, diastole **443**). The ventricular hypertrophy contributes to the heart failure by causing abnormalities of relaxation and filling of the left ventricle. Ao – aorta; LA – left atrium; LV – left ventricle.

444

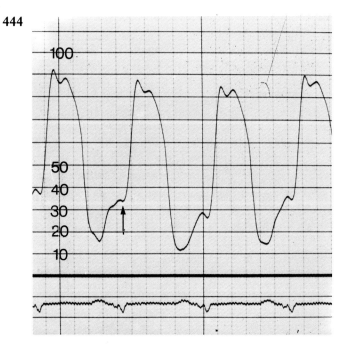

444 Pressure tracing recorded from a patient with hypertensive heart failure. The left ventricular end-diastolic pressure (arrow) is markedly elevated at 35 mmHg.

VI CONGENITAL HEART DISEASE

Breathlessness is a late phenomena in adult congenital heart disease. The commonest cause is an underlying atrial septal defect where a change in atrial rhythm is often the precipitating factor. Ventricular septal defect and patent ductus arteriosus rarely present with breathlessness before the development of the Eisenmenger syndrome. The development of pulmonary hypertension (Eisenmenger syndrome) is associated with cyanosis and later right heart failure.

In later life, severe pulmonary stenosis will cause right heart failure as will Ebstein's anomaly and Uhl's syndrome.

The combination of hypertension and coarctation (possibly with aortic valve disease) occasionally leads to the development of left heart failure. Cor triatriatum is an exceptionally rare condition that leads to pulmonary oedema.

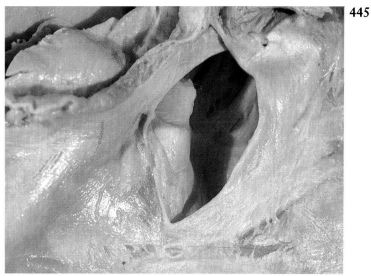

445

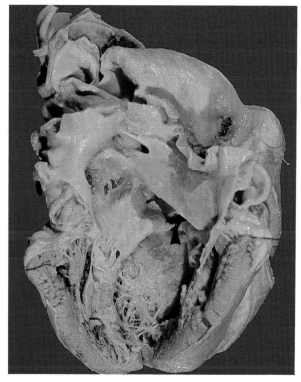

446

445 & 446 Macroscopic view of a secundum atrial septal defect viewed from the left atrium (**445**) and primum atrial septal defect (**446**) (arrowed). The ostium primum defect occurs below the fossa ovalis and involves the atrioventricular valves.

447

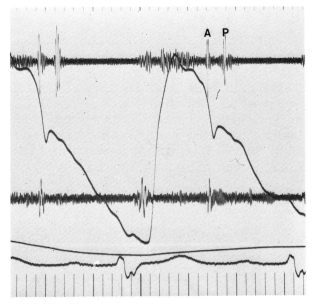

447 Phonocardiogram and carotid pulse showing a systolic murmur and fixed splitting of the second heart sound in an atrial septal defect.

448

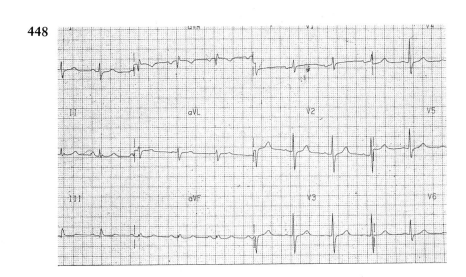

448 Electrocardiogram in secundum atrial septal defect showing sinus rhythm, right bundle branch block and right axis deviation pattern.

449

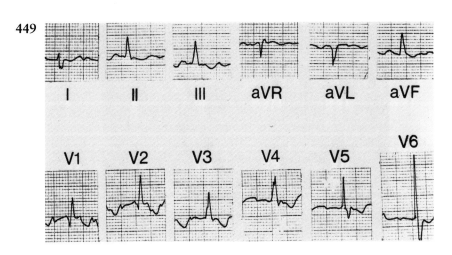

449 Electrocardiogram in secundum atrial septal defect showing atrial flutter with a right bundle branch block and a right axis deviation pattern. It is usually when atrial tachyarrhythmias occur that secundum atrial septal defects present with heart failure.

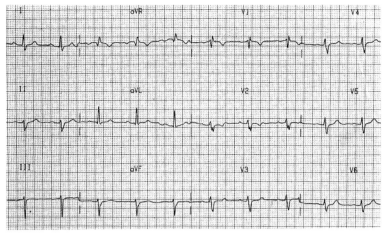

450 Electrocardiogram in primum atrial septal defect showing sinus rhythm with a right bundle branch block and left axis deviation pattern. The electrical axis is the simplest means of distinguishing primum and secundum atrial septal defects.

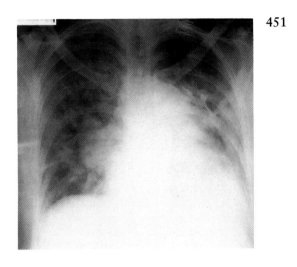

451

451 Chest radiograph in secundum atrial septal defect with heart failure. The heart is grossly enlarged as are the pulmonary arteries; there is severe pulmonary plethora.

452

453

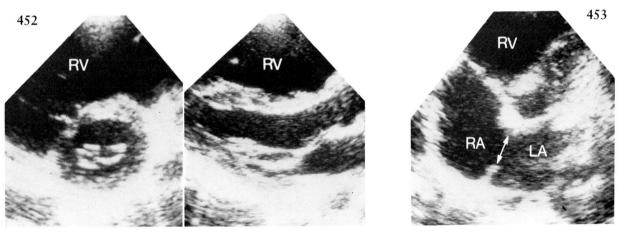

452 & 453 Cross sectional echocardiograms (parasternal short axis **452** (left); long axis **452** (right); apical long axis **453**). The left ventricle is small and the right ventricle (RV) is dilated both in the body and outflow tract. The mitral valve appears to prolapse in systole because of the distortion of the left ventricle and the size of the right ventricular cavity. In the apical view the atrial septal defect (arrow) can be seen as well as the enlargement of the right ventricle and right atrium (RA) compared with the left ventricle and left atrium (LA).

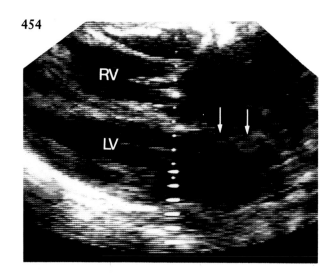

454 Cross sectional echocardiogram in the subcostal view. This is the best view for examining atrial septal defects because the echo beam is at right angles to the defect, as in this example of a secundum atrial septal defect (arrows). LV – left ventricle; RV – right ventricle.

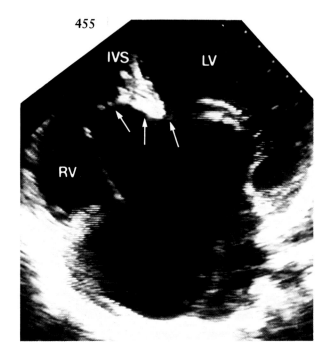

455 Cross sectional echocardiogram (apical long axis view). This primum atrial septal defect exhibits bridging of the atrioventricular valve leaflets with insertion of their apparatus (arrows) into the crest of the interventricular septum (IVS). No portion of the interatrial septum is visualised. LV – left ventricle; RV – right ventricle.

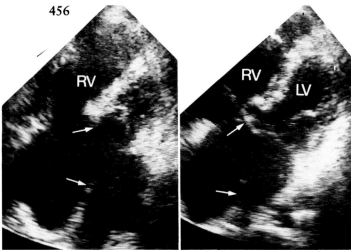

456 Cross sectional echocardiogram (apical long axis view; systole left, diastole right). The motion of the atrioventricular valve is seen in systole and in diastole as well as the defect in the primum region (arrows). LV – left ventricle; RV – right ventricle.

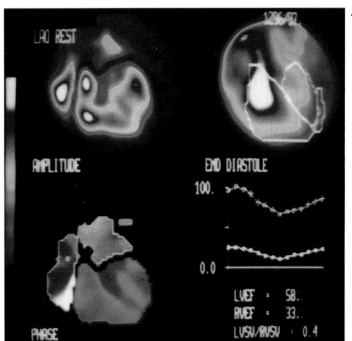

457

457 Gated blood pool scan in atrial septal defect. End-diastolic image (top right) showing a normal sized left ventricle and a dilated right ventricle. Amplitude image (top left) showing normal wall motion of both ventricles and a hyperkinetic right atrium. Phase image (bottom left) showing delayed contraction of the right ventricle. Left and right volume time curves (bottom right) showing left ventricular ejection fraction of 58%, right ventricular ejection fraction 33%, left ventricular stroke volume/right ventricular stroke volume 0.4 indicating the size of the left to the right shunt.

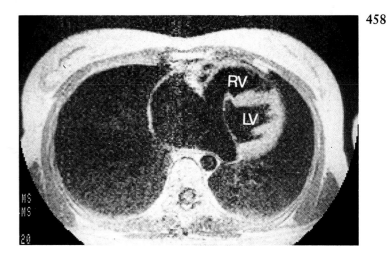

458

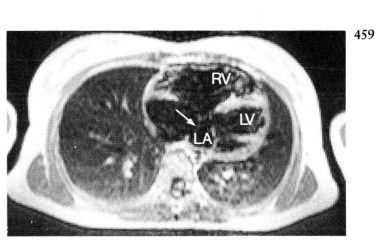

459

458 & 459 Magnetic resonance scans (transverse sections at different levels) showing an atrial septal defect. There is absence of the primum septum (arrow). LA – left atrium; LV – left ventricle; RV – right ventricle.

460

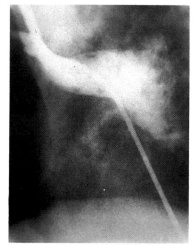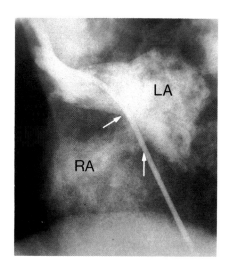

460 Angiocardiogram in secundum atrial septal defect. There has been an injection of contrast into the right upper lobe pulmonary vein with filling of the left atrium (LA). Subsequently there is filling of the right atrium (RA) through the atrial septal defect (arrows).

461

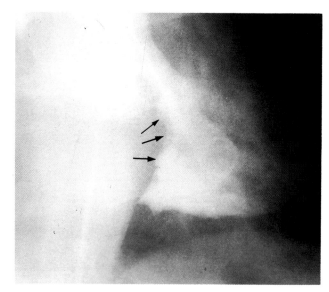

462

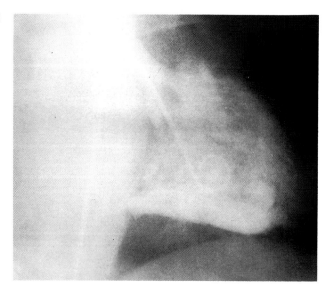

461 & 462 Left ventricular angiogram in atrioventricular canal defect (systole **461**; diastole **462**). There is a typical goose neck deformity seen in the systolic image.

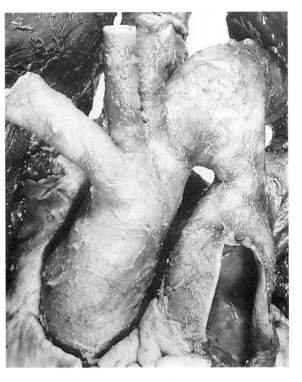

463 Patent ductus arteriosus. The pulmonary artery is seen in the upper part of the figure and the aorta in the lower part.

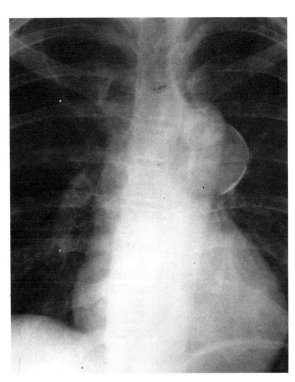

464 Chest radiograph in patent ductus arteriosus showing an enlarged heart with a calcified duct.

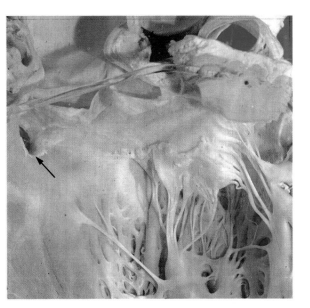

465 Peri-membranous ventricular septal defect (arrow) viewed from the left ventricle.

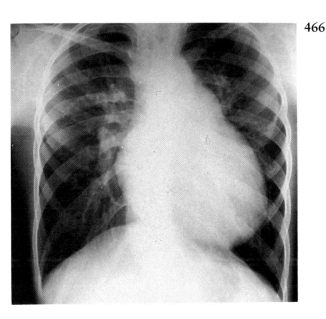

466 Chest radiograph in ventricular septal defect showing an enlarged heart, enlarged pulmonary arteries and pulmonary plethora.

467

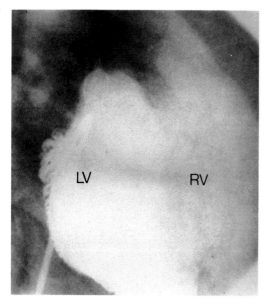

467 Angiocardiogram in ventricular septal defect with injection of the left ventricle (catheter passing via the ventricular septal defect) filling both left and right ventricles (LV, RV).

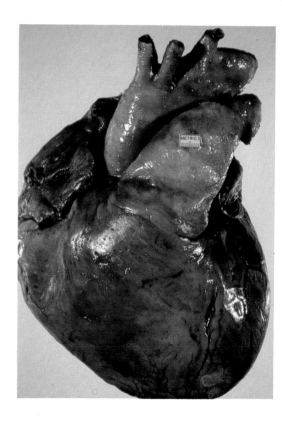

469

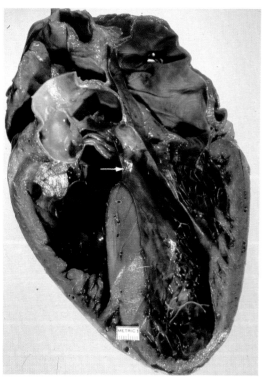

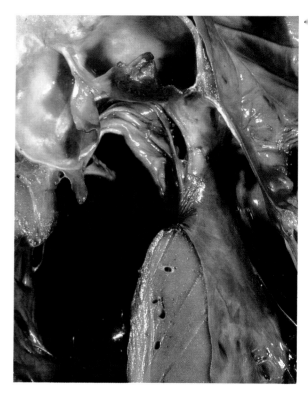

468-470 External appearance of the heart (**468**) of a 63-year-old man who had a large ventricular septal defect with pulmonary hypertension (Eisenmenger syndrome). The right ventricle is large and bulges anteriorly, the pulmonary trunk is very large and wider than the aorta. Long axis section (**469**) showing dilated left and right ventricles with a sub-aortic ventricular septal defect (arrow). Higher power view (**470**) showing the large intramural coronary arteries within the septum.

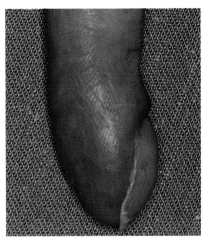

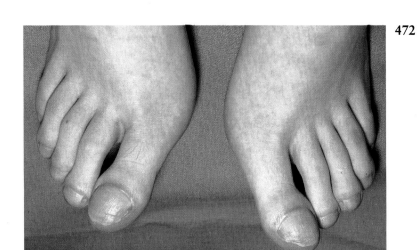

471 Cyanosis and finger clubbing in a patient with an Eisenmenger ventricular septal defect.

472 Cyanosis and digital clubbing will also be seen affecting the toes.

473 Electrocardiogram in Eisenmenger ventricular septal defect showing sinus rhythm with gross right ventricular hypertrophy.

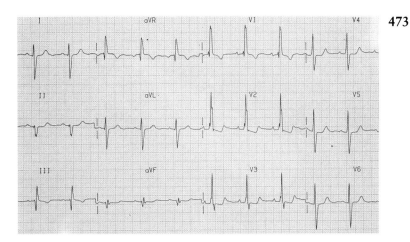

474 Chest radiograph in Eisenmenger ventricular septal defect showing an enlarged heart with calcification of the pulmonary arteries; the pulmonary vasculature appears normal.

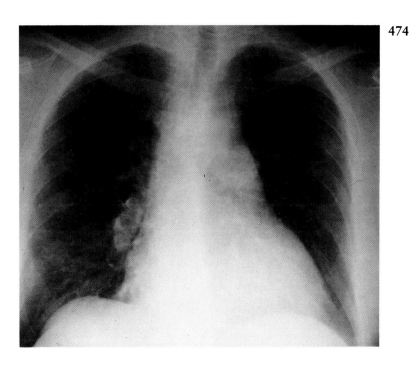

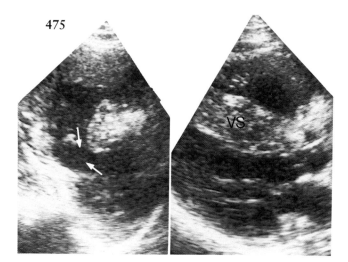

475 Cross sectional echocardiogram (parasternal short axis view left, long axis view right). In Eisenmenger ventricular septal defect there is septal hypertrophy seen in the long axis view (VS) and a large ventricular septal defect in the muscular portion of the septum (arrowed).

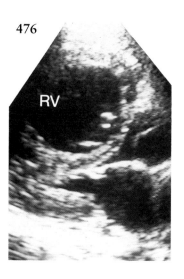

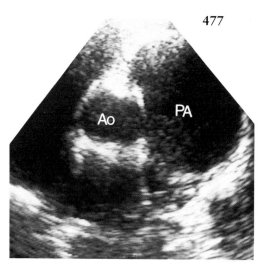

476 & 477 Cross sectional echocardiogram (parasternal long axis view **476**, short axis view **477**) in Eisenmenger patent ductus arteriosus. The left ventricle is small and distorted by the grossly dilated right ventricle. The pulmonary artery (PA) is enormously enlarged in comparison to the aorta (AO). RV – right ventricle.

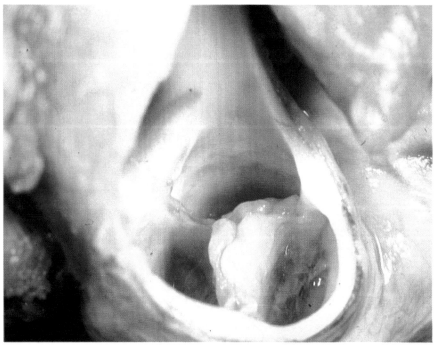

478 Stenosed pulmonary valve viewed from above.

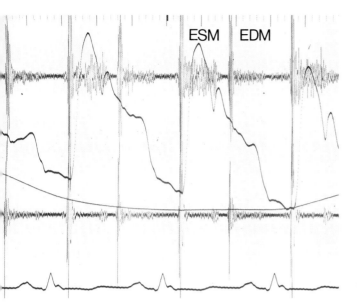

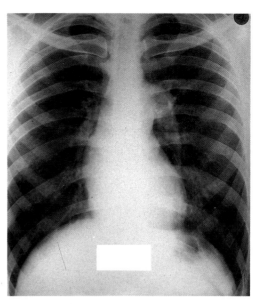

479 Phonocardiogram and carotid pulse in pulmonary stenosis showing a loud pulmonary systolic ejection murmur (ESM). Pulmonary closure is delayed and soft and in addition, there is an early diastolic murmur (EDM) due to pulmonary regurgitation.

480 Chest radiograph in severe pulmonary stenosis. There is a prominent pulmonary artery due to post stenotic dilatation.

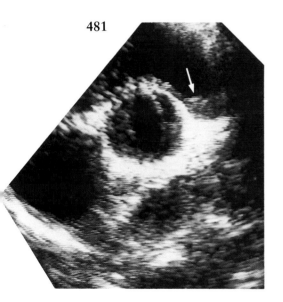

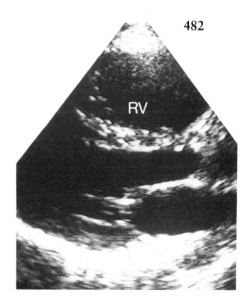

481 & 482 Cross sectional echocardiogram (parasternal short axis view **481**, long axis view **482**) in a patient with severe pulmonary valve stenosis. In the short axis view the pulmonary valve is thick and can be seen to dome while moving (arrow). The body of the right ventricle (RV) is dilated although the outflow tract is of normal size.

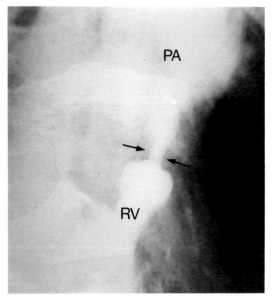

483 Right ventricular (RV) angiogram (lateral projection) showing a stenosed pulmonary valve and gross post stenotic pulmonary artery (PA) dilatation with a narrow jet of contrast passing through the valve (arrows).

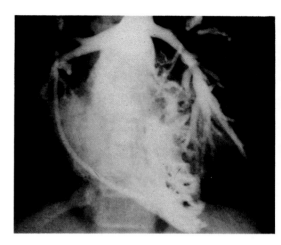

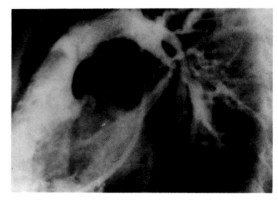

484 Right ventricular angiogram in branch pulmonary stenosis showing a normal main pulmonary artery, but stenosis of the peripheral pulmonary arteries.

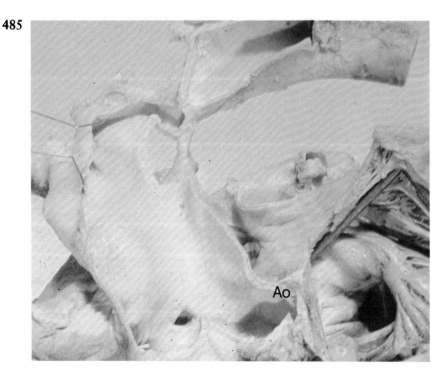

485 Coarctation (arrowed) of the aorta (AO) is present between the origin of the large left subclavian artery and the site of attachment of a closed ductus arteriosus.

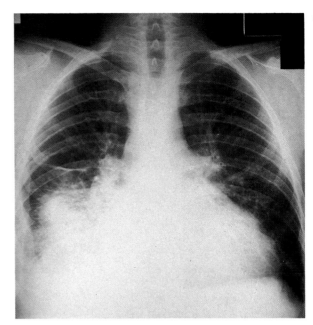

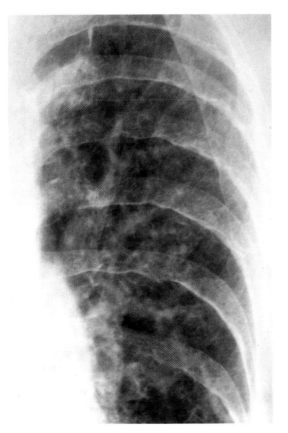

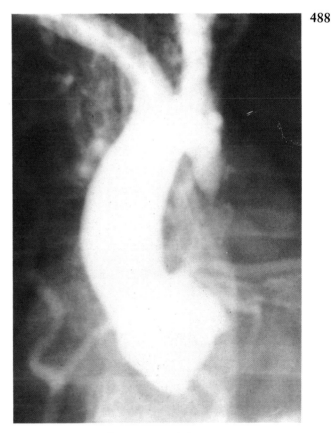

486 & 487 Chest radiograph in coarctation with heart failure showing a grossly enlarged heart, pulmonary oedema and rib notching (**486**). Rib notching is shown in close up (**487**).

488 Aortogram showing an adult coarctation.

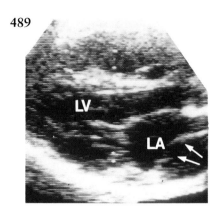
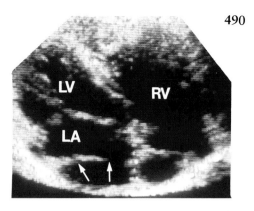

489 & 490 Cross sectional echocardiograms (parasternal long axis view **489**, apical long axis view **490**) in cor triatriatum. There is a membrane lying within the left atrium (LA) (arrow) above which the pulmonary veins drain. This leads to physical signs similar to mitral stenosis. LV – left ventricle; RV – right ventricle.

491

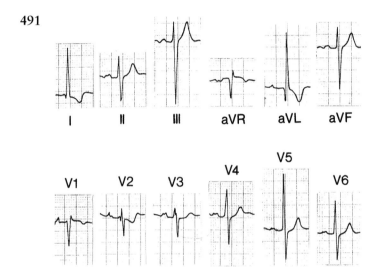

491 Electrocardiogram in Ebstein's anomaly typically shows an interatrial conduction defect and incomplete right bundle branch block with left axis deviation.

492

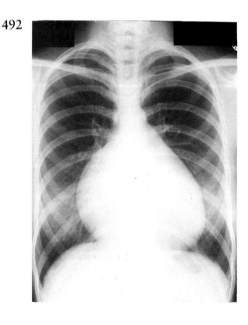

492 Chest radiograph in Ebstein's anomaly showing an enlarged heart, due to an enlarged right atrium with oligaemia of the lung fields.

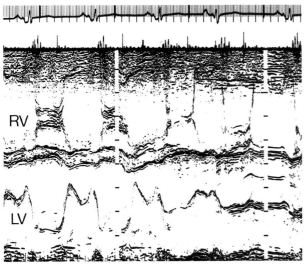

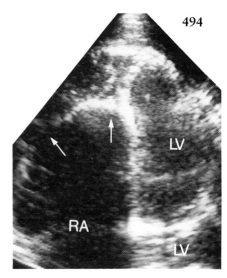

493 & 494 Echocardiograms in Ebstein's anomaly. The M-mode echocardiogram (**493**) shows the right ventricle to be dilated and the tricuspid valve to be prominent. The closure of the tricuspid valve follows mitral valve closure which is the reverse of normal. The apical long axis view echocardiogram (**494**) shows the mitral valve to be in a normal position, with the right atrium occupying a major portion of the right ventricular cavity. The tricuspid valve (arrow) is displaced downwards towards the apex of the right ventricle and is abnormal in appearance. LA – left atrium; LV – left ventricle; RA – right atrium; RV – right ventricle.

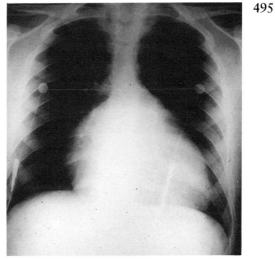

495 Chest radiograph in Uhl's anomaly. This shows cardiac enlargement particularly of the right atrium with oligaemia of the lung fields.

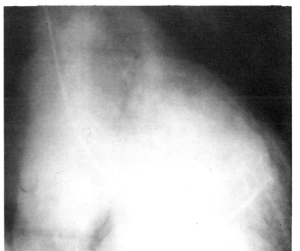

496 Right ventricular angiogram in Uhl's anomaly. This shows the right ventricle to be grossly enlarged and thin walled with loss of trabeculation.

VII RIGHT HEART FAILURE

Acute right heart failure

Acute right heart failure may occur due to an inferior myocardial infarction involving the right ventricle or following a large pulmonary embolus. In the case of massive pulmonary embolism the patient usually collapses suddenly and becomes shocked. Pulmonary infarction rarely causes acute right heart failure but may proceed a massive pulmonary embolism. It is therefore important to diagnose even small pulmonary emboli early so that appropriate treatment can be instigated; the investigation of choice is ventilation perfusion scanning. Pulmonary embolism may be confused with the adult respiratory distress syndrome which may also cause acute heart failure, this occurs particularly following road traffic accidents or after surgery.

Chronic right heart failure will occur secondary to left heart failure, tricuspid and pulmonary valvular lesions, ischaemic damage to the right ventricle, cardiomyopathies involving predominantly the right ventricle and congenital heart lesions (see earlier sections). Heart failure is an important late sequalae in pulmonary hypertension. The most common cause in the UK is probably chronic obstructive airways disease, but other causes that should be considered include primary pulmonary hypertension, thrombo-embolic disease, disorders of ventilation such as scoliosis and obesity and finally the very rare pulmonary veno-occlusive disease.

Investigation of chronic right heart failure should be directed to identifying the underlying cause.

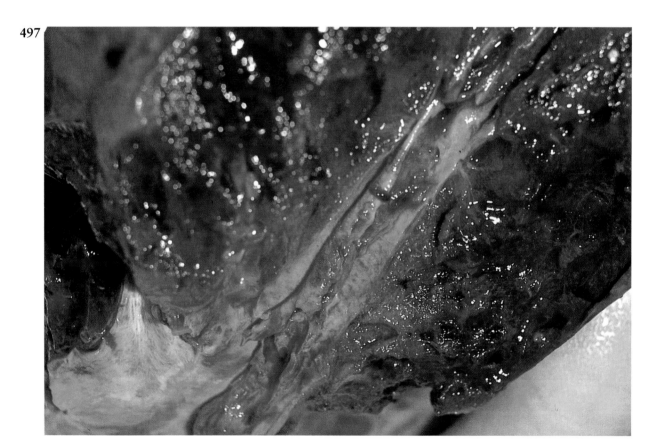

497 Pathology of massive pulmonary embolism. Opened lung in a patient who died of a massive pulmonary embolism. The left main pulmonary artery can be seen filled with an embolus.

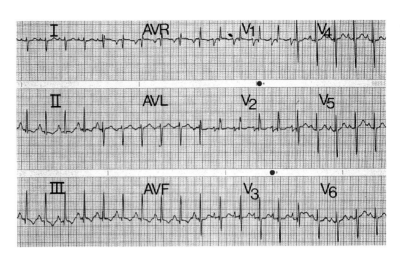

498 The electrocardiogram in pulmonary embolism may be normal or show a variety of abnormalities. Commonest, is said to be the presence of S1, Q3, T3. This is a response to increased right heart pressures and raising of the diaphragm. Alternatively, the electrocardiographic pattern of acute cor pulmonale may be seen, as in this example, with right atrial enlargement (tall peaked P waves in the inferior leads) and right axis deviation.

499

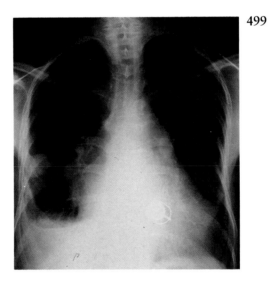

499 There are a variety of radiographic appearances in patients with pulmonary embolism. In the presence of massive pulmonary embolism the chest x-ray may be normal or there may be the appearance of pulmonary oligaemia. The more usual appearances are of pulmonary infarction shown here as a wedge-shaped peripheral shadow in the right mid-zone in a patient with a Starr-Edwards mitral valve replacement.

500

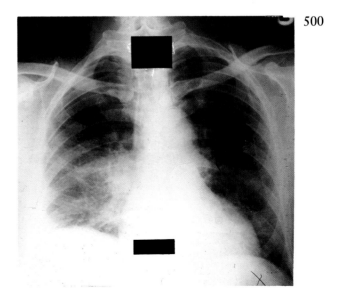

500 Chest radiograph showing pulmonary infarction and embolism resulting in pleural effusions and a raised hemidiaphragm.

VENTILATION   PERFUSION

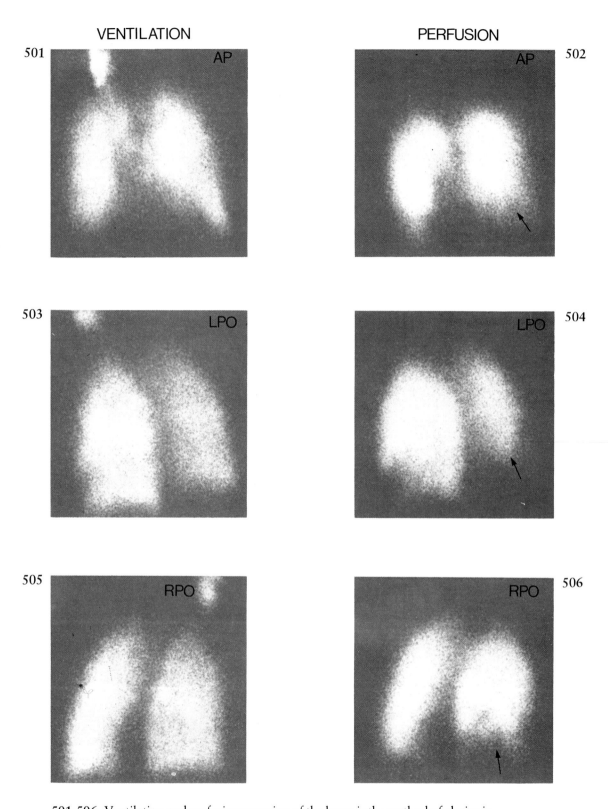

501-506 Ventilation and perfusion scanning of the lungs is the method of choice in diagnosing pulmonary embolism. Perfusion scanning will reveal defects in the presence of a normal ventilation scan. Ventilation (502, 503, 505) and perfusion (501, 504, 506) scans in pulmonary embolism. There is a defect in the left lower zone in the perfusion scan; the ventilation scan is normal.

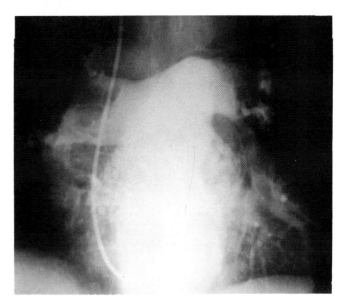

507 Pulmonary arteriogram in pulmonary embolism showing a large filling defect in the left pulmonary artery.

508

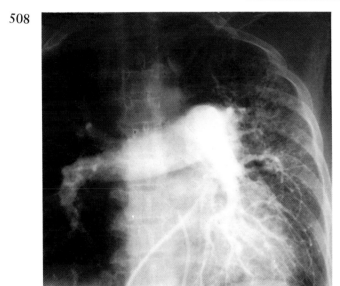

509

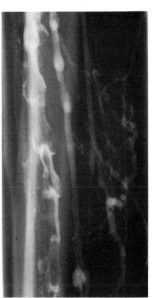

508 & 509 Pulmonary arteriogram in pulmonary embolism showing that the pulmonary blood flow to the left upper zone is markedly diminished (508). This resulted in a pulmonary infarction as opposed to 507 which resulted in shock. The source of the pulmonary embolism was from the deep veins of the leg shown on the venogram as multiple filling defects (509).

510

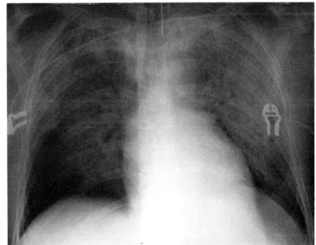

510 Chest radiograph in adult respiratory distress syndrome showing gross opacification of the lungs.

Chronic right heart failure

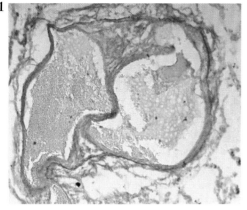

511 Microscopic section of the lung in thrombo-embolic disease causing pulmonary hypertension with grade IV arteriolar dilation.

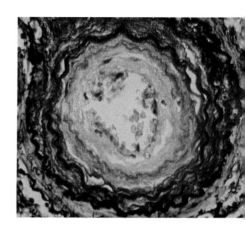

512 Histology of pulmonary artery in secondary pulmonary hypertension, showing splitting of the internal elastic lamina and intimal fibrosis.

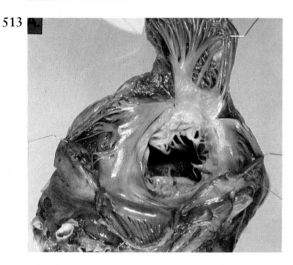

513 Opened heart showing a dilated right ventricle and tricuspid valve, in a patient with pulmonary hypertension and heart failure.

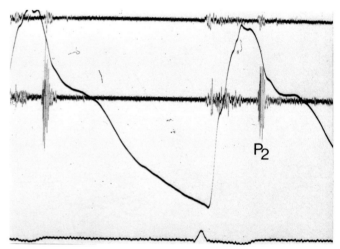

514 Simultaneous phonocardiogram and carotid pulse showing a loud pulmonary closure sound (P_2) in primary pulmonary hypertension.

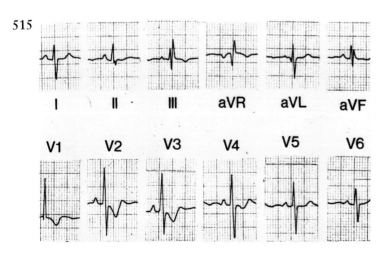

515 Electrocardiogram in primary pulmonary hypertension showing gross right ventricular hypertrophy.

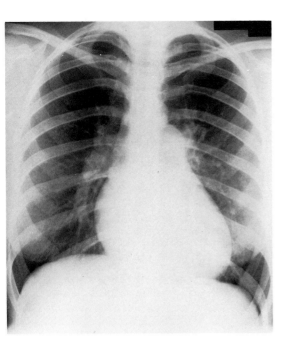

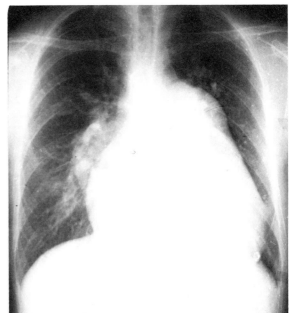

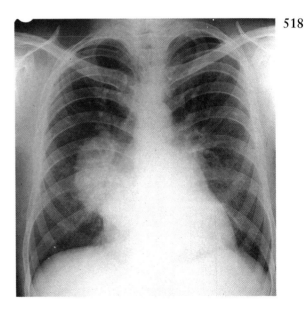

516-518 Chest radiographs in primary pulmonary hypertension showing the different stages of the disease process. Initially, the chest radiograph is almost normal with the exception of dilatation of the main pulmonary artery (**516**), later there is gross dilatation of the main pulmonary artery (**517**) with cardiomegaly. Finally, almost at the end stage of the disease, there may be aneurysmal dilatation of the main pulmonary artery (**518**).

519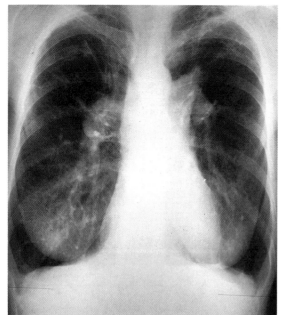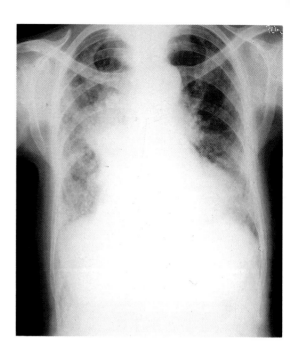

521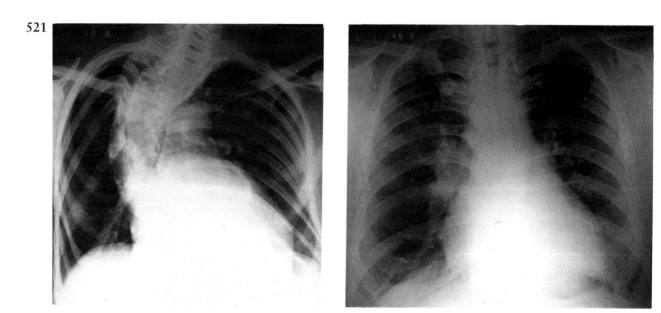

519-522 Chest radiographs in secondary causes of pulmonary hypertension. The chest radiograph may suggest the underlying cause and in these examples there is chronic obstructive airways disease with emphysema and pulmonary artery dilatation (**519**) and fibrosing alveolitis with diffuse lung fibrosis (**520**). Scoliosis may lead to pulmonary hypertension due to the chronic hypercapnia (**521**) and by a similar mechanism, gross obesity may lead to pulmonary hypertension (**522**).

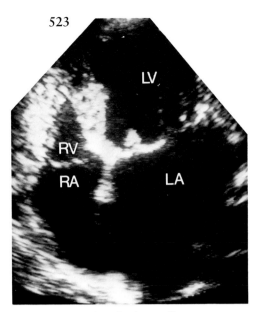

523

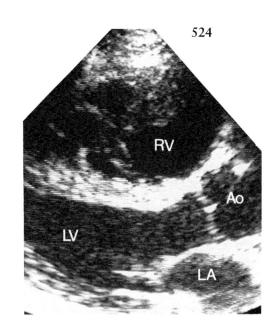

524

523 Cross sectional echocardiogram (apical four chamber view) in pulmonary hypertension showing gross right ventricular hypertrophy. Note the right atrium is not enlarged. LA – left atrium; LV – left ventricle. RA – right atrium; RV – right ventricle.

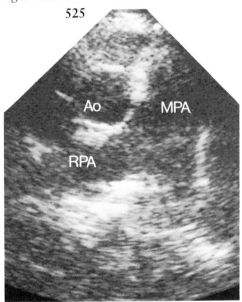

525

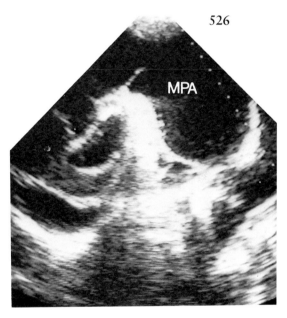

526

524 & 525 Cross sectional echocardiogram (parasternal long axis view **524**, short axis view **525**) in pulmonary hypertension. The right ventricle is enlarged and the left ventricle and atrium are normal (**524**). The aortic root (AO) is of normal size (AO) but the main pulmonary artery (MPA) is enlarged and both right (RPA) and left pulmonary arteries are dilated (**525**).

526 Cross sectional echocardiogram (parasternal short axis view) in pulmonary hypertension showing gross dilatation of the main pulmonary artery (MPA).

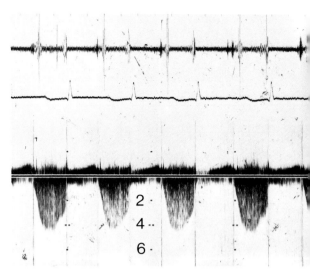

527 M-mode echocardiogram in primary pulmonary hypertension showing a grossly enlarged right ventricle with increased excursion of the tricuspid valve (TV).

528 Continuous wave Doppler echocardiogram (apical view) in pulmonary hypertension. The peak velocity of Doppler derived tricuspid regurgitation is equal to the right ventricular systolic pressure. In this example, this exceeds 4 M/s suggesting a right ventricular systolic pressure in excess of 64 mmHg.

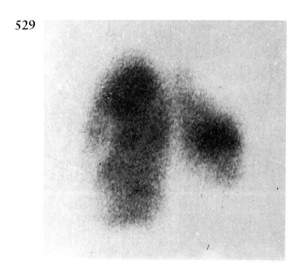

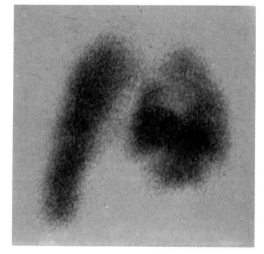

529 & 530 Perfusion lung scans in left posterior oblique projection (529) and right posterior oblique projection (530) in pulmonary hypertension showing multiple filling defects due to multiple small pulmonary emboli.

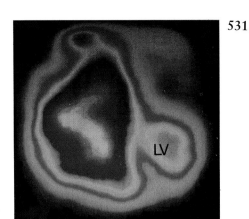

531 Gated blood pool scan showing a dilated right ventricle at end-diastole with a normal sized left ventricle (LV) in a patient with pulmonary hypertension.

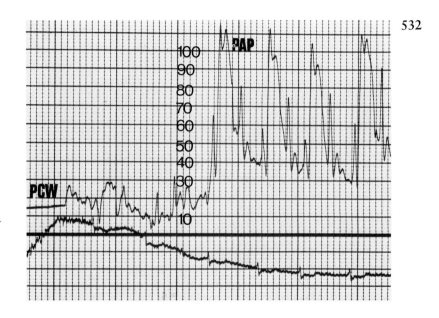

532 Haemodynamic trace in primary pulmonary hypertension. Pulmonary capillary wedge pressure (PCW) is normal and on withdrawal, the pulmonary artery (PAP) is grossly elevated.

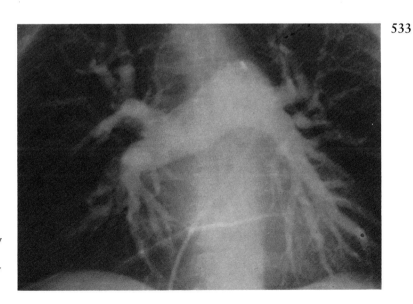

533 Pulmonary arteriogram in primary pulmonary hypertension. This shows dilatation of the main pulmonary artery and peripheral pruning.

534

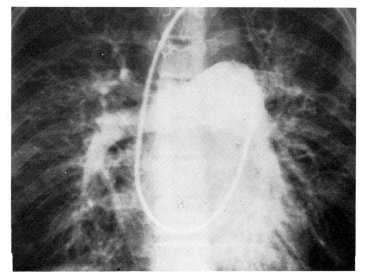

534 Pulmonary arteriogram in pulmonary hypertension due to chronic obstructive airways disease. This shows the pulmonary vasculature to be essentially normal.

535

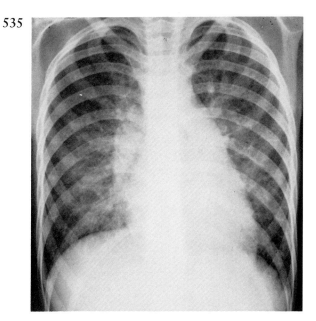

535 Chest radiograph in veno-occlusive disease showing a small heart with severe pulmonary oedema.

536

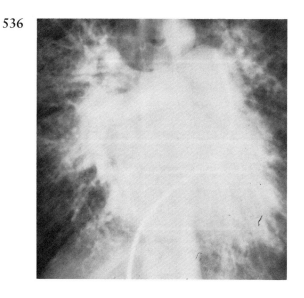

536 Pulmonary arteriogram in veno-occlusive disease showing the pulmonary vasculature to be grossly abnormal with markedly dilated pulmonary arterioles. This is due to progressive narrowing and fibrotic occlusion of the pulmonary vein and venules.

VIII OTHER CAUSES OF HEART FAILURE

High output failure

Heart failure may occasionally occur in the presence of normal left and right ventricular function due to a high cardiac output. The most common of these include severe anaemia and thyrotoxicosis. In developing countries Beri-Beri should be consi- dered. Arteriovenous fistulae which may be large as in pulmonary arteriovenous fistulae or multiple and small as in Paget's disease, are rare causes of heart failure.

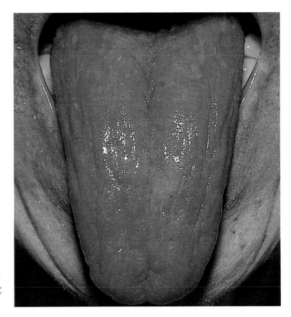

537

537 A beefy tongue is shown in a patient with pernicious anaemia. The haemaglobin was 4 g/dl and and the patient presented with shortness of breath and angina.

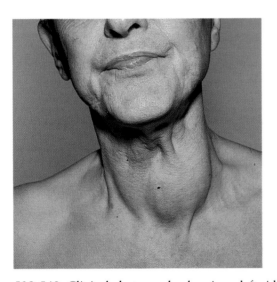

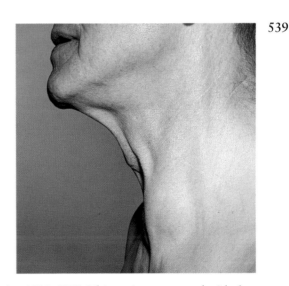

539

538-540 Clinical photographs showing a left-sided thyroid goitre (538, 539). This patient presented with the symptoms of thyrotoxicosis and in addition was short of breath. The thyroid scan (540) shows a large filling defect on the left side.

540

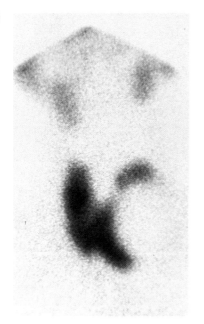

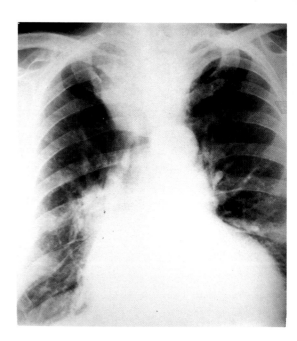

541 Chest radiograph in thyroid heart failure showing a large thyroid which has extended retrosternally together with evidence of pulmonary oedema and cardiomegaly.

542

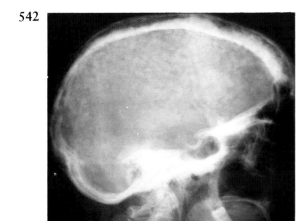

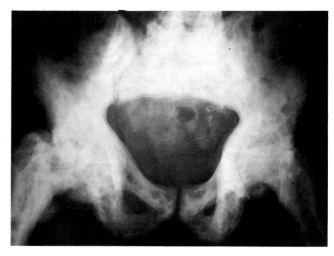

542-545 Radiographs of the skull (**542**), the pelvis (**543**) and the femur (**544**) in Paget's disease. This shows the skull vault to be greatly thickened and fluffy in appearance and replacement of the normal bony architecture by coarse abnormal looking trabeculae; enlargement of the external contours of the bone and Looser's zones at the end of the long bones. The chest x-ray (**545**) shows an enlarged heart and pulmonary congestion.

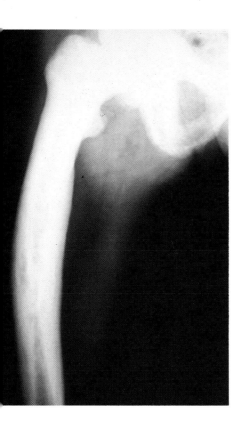

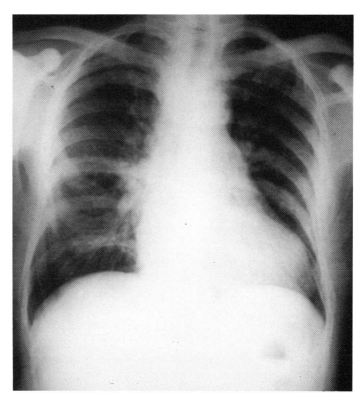

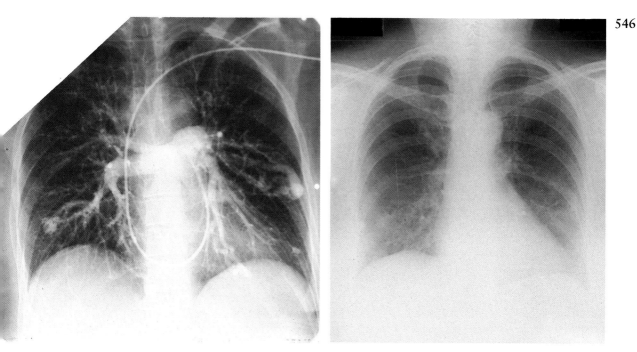

546 Chest radiograph (right) in pulmonary arteriovenous fistulae. The chest radiograph shows slight enlargement of the heart with pulmonary congestion. A shadow in the right lower zone is the site of a fistula confirmed by pulmonary arteriography (left).

Pericardial disease

Cardiac tamponade and restrictive pericarditis may both give the physical signs and symptoms of right heart failure and in addition, pulmonary congestion may occasionally occur. The diagnosis is made on chest x-ray, echocardiography and confirmed by haemodynamics. Constrictive pericarditis must be distinguished from restrictive cardiomyopathy because of the different therapeutic implications.

547

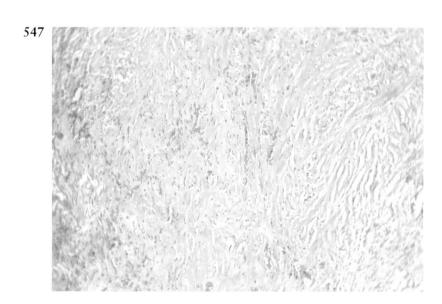

547 Microscopic section showing a thickened, fibrous pericardium in constrictive pericarditis.

548

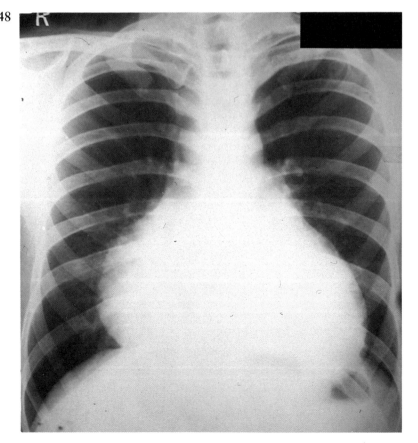

548 Chest radiograph showing an enlarged rounded heart due to a large tuberculous pericardial effusion.

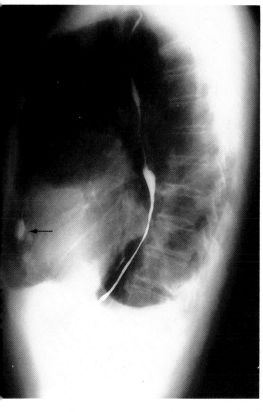

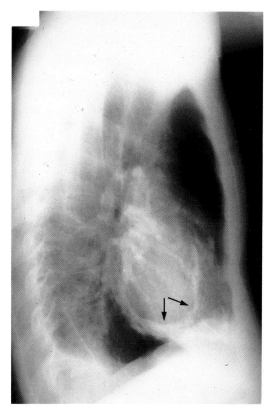

549 & 550 Chest radiographs showing localised (**549**) and generalised (**550**) calcification (arrowed) of the pericardium. These patients both had constrictive pericarditis, an important cause of which is tuberculosis.

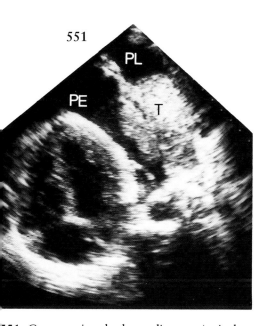

551 Cross sectional echocardiogram (apical long axis view) in a patient with a pericardial tumour and cardiac tamponade. The heart is normal, but there is a large pericardial effusion (PE) as well as a pleural effusion (PL). The tumour (T) can be seen attached to the pericardium.

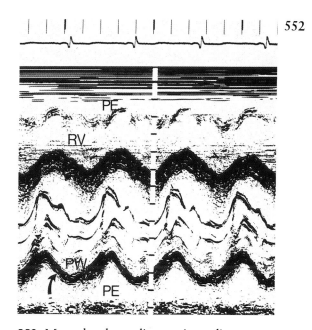

552 M-mode echocardiogram in cardiac tamponade showing a pericardial effusion (PE) both anterior and posterior to the heart. Abnormal motion of both right and left ventricles is seen. PW – posterior wall; RV – right ventricle.

553

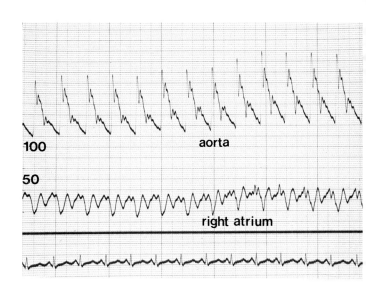

553 M-mode echocardiogram showing thickening of the posterior pericardium (arrows). The initial diastolic filling of the left ventricle (LV) is abnormal suggesting the presence of constriction. PW – posterior wall; VS – ventricular septum.

555

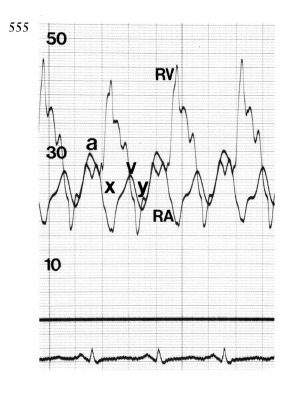

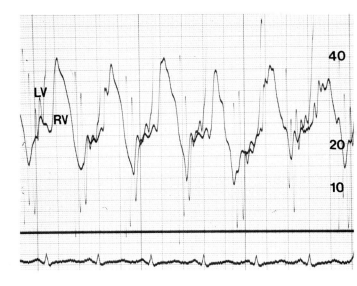

554-556 Haemodynamic traces in constrictive pericarditis showing a marked increase in the systolic arterial pressure on inspiration (**554**); this is pulsus paradoxus. Simultaneous right atrial and right ventricular pressures show a raised right atrial pressure with a rapid x and y descent (**555**). Simultaneous right ventricular and left ventricular pressures show the end-diastolic pressures of both ventricles to be the same (**556**); there is also a 'dip and plateau' to the pressure wave form.

Cardiac tumours

Cardiac tumours are rare but often present with heart failure. By far the commonest is left atrial myxoma that causes obstruction of the mitral valve. Much more rarely, atrial myxomas may involve the right atrium when obstruction of the tricuspid valve will occur. Very rarely, primary tumours of the heart involving the right and left ventricle produce restriction of ventricular filling. The diagnosis is made by cross sectional echocardiography.

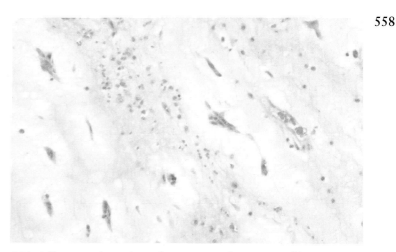

558 Microscopic section of a myxoma showing weakly eosinophilic and basophilic matrix.

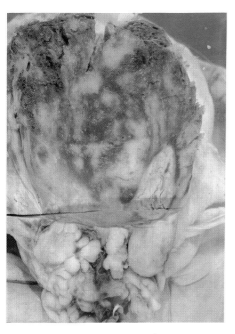

557 Macroscopic section showing an atrial myxoma through the opened wall of the left atrium. There are islands of pale mucoid tissue within the mass of the tumour.

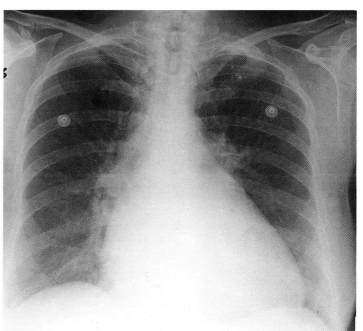

559 Chest radiograph in left atrial myxoma showing a 'mitralised' heart; an enlarged left atrium, a prominent left atrial appendage and upper lobe blood diversion can be seen.

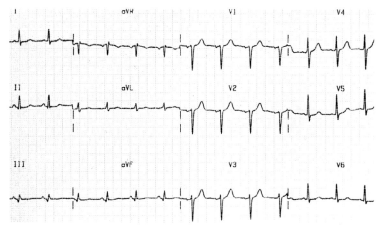

560 Electrocardiogram showing left atrial enlargement due to a left atrial myxoma.

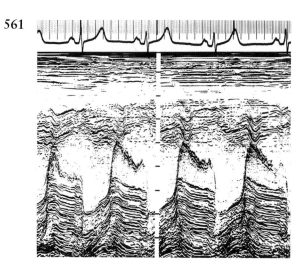

561 M-mode echocardiogram showing a left atrial myxoma. The mitral valve motion is abnormal in diastole and multiple linear echoes are seen prolapsing behind it due to the movement of the tumour.

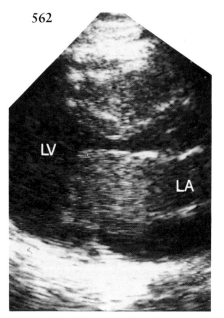

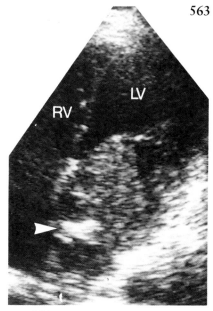

562 & 563 Cross sectional echocardiogram in left atrial myxoma (parasternal long axis view **562**, apical long axis view **563**). The myxoma is seen lying within the left atrium prolapsing through the mitral valve. The tumour can be seen to be attached to the interatrial septum in the region of the foramen ovale (arrow).
LA – left atrium; LV – left ventricle; RV – right ventricle.

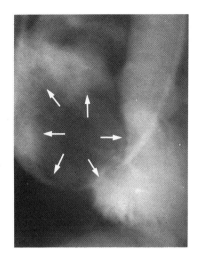

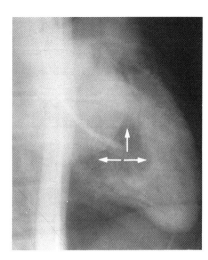

564 Left ventricular angiogram (systole left; diastole right) showing the myxoma in the left atrium during systole and prolapsing into the left ventricle during diastole (arrows).

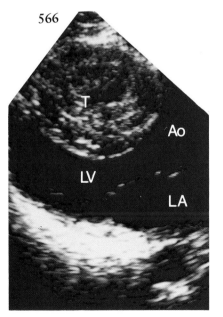

565 Electrocardiogram in a primary right ventricular tumour that presented with right heart failure. There is evidence of right ventricular hypertrophy and right axis deviation.

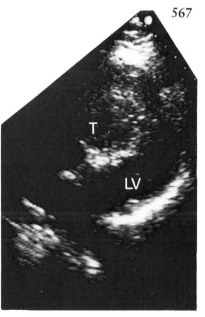

566 & 567 Cross sectional echocardiogram (parasternal long axis view **566**, apical long axis view **567**) in a patient with a right ventricular tumour. A large mass of tissue (T) is seen lying within the interventricular septum and right ventricle. The left ventricle appeared normal. AO – aorta; LA – left atrium; LV – left ventricle.

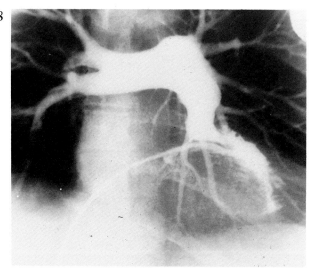

568

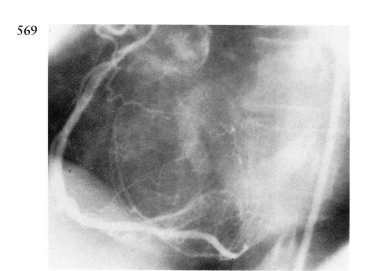

569

568 & 569 Right ventricular angiogram (**568**) showing the tumour as a large filling defect. The right coronary arteriogram (**569**) in the same patient shows there is a tumour circulation.

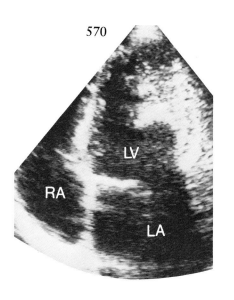

570

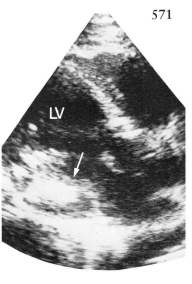

571

570 & 571 Cross sectional echocardiogram (parasternal long axis view **570**, apical long axis view **571**) in a patient with a calcified left ventricular tumour (arrow). A mass of calcium associated with the tumour is seen in the free wall and posterior wall of the left ventricle. The patient presented with cardiac failure. LA – left atrium; LV – left ventricle; RA – right atrium.

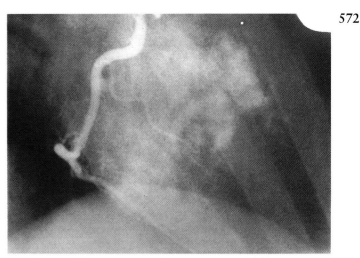

572

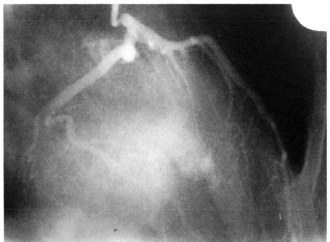

573

572 & 573 Coronary arteriogram in the same patient as in 570, 571 showing the calcification in the left ventricle in relationship to the coronary arteries (right coronary artery 572; left coronary artery 573).

574

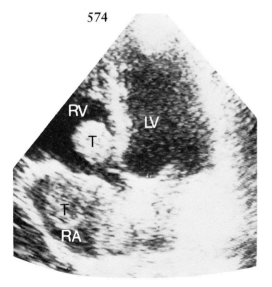

574 Cross sectional echocardiogram (apical long axis view) in metastatic renal hypernephroma. Large tumour masses (T) are seen within the right atrium (RA) prolapsing into the right ventricle (RV); these obstructed venous return and the patient presented with heart failure. LV – left ventricle.

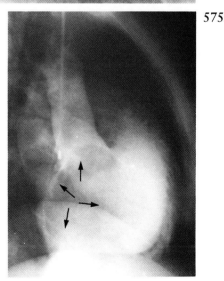

575

575 Right atrial angiogram in right atrial myxoma showing the tumour as a filling defect in the atrium.

INDEX

INDEX

All figures refer to page numbers

Doppler ultrasound   22, 48, 49, 60, 82, 96, 100, 107, 108, 110, 116, 172
Drug addiction   50, 93

Ebstein's anomaly   93, 149, 162, 163
Ehlers Danlos   53, 73
Eisenmenger syndrome   149, 156-158
Electrocardiogram   12, 15, 16, 21, 25, 30, 37, 55, 77, 80, 94, 105, 113, 114, 118, 122, 123, 134, 137, 138, 140, 145, 150, 151, 157, 162, 165, 168, 182, 183
Emphysema   170
Endomyocardial fibrosis   139
Eosinophilia   139, 141-143
Erythema nodosum   125
Extension of myocardial infarction   15

False channel   51
Fibre disarray   134, 145
Fibrosing alveolitis   170
Flail mitral valve   22
Friedreich's ataxia   128

Gallop rhythm   9, 11, 139
Gated blood pool scan   33, 40, 62, 90, 118, 153, 173
Gumma   73

Haemosiderosis   78, 79
Heart muscle disease   9, 111-143
Hepatic congestion   10
Hepatomegaly   139
High arched palate   65
High output state   9, 175-177
Homograft aortic valve replacement   49
Hurler's syndrome   125
Hypernephroma   185
Hypertension   9, 127, 129, 144-149
Hypertrophic cardiomyopathy   128, 132-138, 144

Infective endocarditis   43-50, 93, 98
Infective vegetations   43, 47, 49, 50
Intracardiac shunt   26, 27
Ischaemic heart disease   9, 12-42 -42

Jaundice   10

Jugular venous pressure   9, 11

Left atrial enlargement   76, 77, 79, 81, 82, 84, 90, 95, 113, 123, 139
Left atrial myxoma   181-183
Left atrial thrombus   29, 37-39, 76, 79, 82, 85, 103, 112, 116
Left ventricular aneurysm   29-35
Left ventricular angiogram   13, 19, 24, 28, 34, 41, 50, 63, 85, 91, 92, 108, 109, 120, 137, 153, 156, 157, 183
Left ventricular calcification   31
Left ventricular dilatation   17-19, 41, 53, 59-62, 75, 88, 90, 91, 99, 103, 111-116, 118, 119, 128, 129, 136, 139, 144, 146, 156
Left ventricular end diastolic pressure   41, 48
Left ventricular false aneurysm   32, 33
Left ventricular hypertrophy   53-55, 59, 61, 75, 87, 111, 119, 129, 132-134, 138, 141, 144-148
Left ventricular outflow tract gradient   137-138
Left ventricular scar   15
Left ventricular thrombus   18, 19
Left ventricular tumour   184
Low output state   25

Malar flush   76
Marfans syndrome   53, 64-67
Magnetic resonance imaging   34, 40, 61, 84, 90, 119, 137, 142, 147, 148, 151
Mitral valve
– calcification   79, 81
– chronic disease   53, 76-93
– flail   22
– gradient   84
– prolapse   76, 86-91, 96, 102, 103, 151
– repair   98, 102, 103
– regurgitation   12, 13, 20-25, 46, 50, 76, 80, 87, 92, 98, 103, 108, 109, 116
Mitral valve replacement
– Björk-Shiley   50
– Braunwald-Cutter   106, 109
– facia lata   104, 106-108
– Starr-Edwards   44, 48, 104, 105, 109
– xenograph   43, 48, 106-108
Mitral valve replacement in hypertrophic cardiomyopathy   132, 138
Mitral ring calcification   92
Mitral stenosis
– congenital   82
– rheumatic   76, 85, 94, 95, 98, 100-102, 106-108